OXFORD
INDIA SHORT
INTRODUCTIONS

WATER RESOURCES
OF INDIA

The Oxford India Short
Introductions are concise,
stimulating, and accessible guides
to different aspects of India.
Combining authoritative analysis,
new ideas, and diverse perspectives,
they discuss subjects which are
topical yet enduring, as also
emerging areas of study and debate.

OTHER TITLES IN THE SERIES

OXFORD
INDIA SHORT
INTRODUCTIONS

WATER
RESOURCES
OF INDIA

A. VAIDYANATHAN

OXFORD
UNIVERSITY PRESS

OXFORD
UNIVERSITY PRESS

Oxford University Press is a department of the University of Oxford.
It furthers the University's objective of excellence in research, scholarship,
and education by publishing worldwide. Oxford is a registered trademark of
Oxford University Press in the UK and in certain other countries

Published in India by
Oxford University Press
YMCA Library Building, 1 Jai Singh Road, New Delhi 110001, India

ISBN-13: 978-0-19-809042-7
ISBN-10: 0-19-809042-0

Typeset in 11/15.6 Bembo Std
by Excellent Laser Typesetters, Pitampura, Delhi 110 034
Printed in India at G.H. Prints Pvt Ltd, New Delhi 110 020

Contents

Tables

Preface

The world is facing a serious, and worsening, global water crisis. So is India. Its signs manifest in the increasingly widespread incidence of water scarcity and conflict, the depletion of groundwater, the deterioration of the environment, and the pollution of water sources. People and communities experiencing the impact of these on their lives and livelihood are naturally more concerned about coping with their immediate problems rather than with their larger dimensions and societal implications. Policymakers, planners, and the political class also tend to view these problems in short-term perspectives, and look for piecemeal solutions for particular uses and in particular regions, unmindful of the fact that their different manifestations and underlying causes are interrelated.

Effective solutions need to address the complexity of the problems relating to water, and be dealt with in integrated and holistic ways. This monograph presents such a perspective.

Overall supply of freshwater from rainfall, both directly and indirectly, contributes to renewable supplies of surface water and groundwater. The necessity for tapping these renewable supplies arises because climatic conditions (reflected in the quantum and reliability of rainfall, temperatures, and their seasonal distribution) make effective availability from local precipitation limit the kinds of crops that can be grown and their yields. The supplies are also inadequate to meet domestic and non-agricultural requirements for a growing population. The monograph, therefore, begins with an explanation of the determinants of freshwater supply.

The water needs for agriculture depends on the climate, and the demand for food and fibre; the requirement for non-agricultural uses is a function of the degree of industrialization and urbanization. Both, especially the requirements for non-agricultural uses, increase with growth of population and incomes. The potential for tapping renewable supplies depends on the magnitude of surface water and groundwater resources.

The extent to which they can be tapped is constrained by technology, the capacity to mobilize investment (and manage it on a large scale), and considerations of economic viability. The existence of vast variations across and within countries in all these respects, and their underlying factors, are highlighted.

India's need to tap renewable supplies for agriculture is greater as compared to both countries in temperate climates and in East Asia because of its hot climate and the high seasonal concentration of rainfall, which is preceded and followed by long dry seasons. The demand for domestic and non-agricultural uses, though relatively small now, is growing rapidly. However, water needs, regional differences in climate and terrain, sub-surface geology, and the potential for renewable supplies of surface water and groundwater vary widely across regions.

Historically, available technology permitted only the limited use of renewable supplies. Being largely determined by the local climate as well as by the proximity to streams and natural storages, the productivity of land remained very low, and variable. It is only in the second half of the twentieth century that a combination of the increasing requirements of a growing population, technological advances, and government strategies to exploit land for increasing food production led to the rapid utilization of water supply from large-scale storages, canal systems, and groundwater.

The key elements of this strategy—its outcome in terms of the increase in the volume of additional water from the surface and the ground, and the growth of irrigated area and overall agricultural production—are recounted in some detail. The spread of irrigation, combined with improvements in agricultural technology, played a key role in transforming this sector from one of near stagnation to one of sustained—and historically unprecedented—growth in the early decades after Independence. It also accounts for the bulk increase in output. However, currently, the increase in irrigated crop yields—both per hectare and per unit of water consumed—is, by all accounts, much below the attainable potential due to many factors: the underutilization of the capacity of surface systems, the wasteful use of water actually supplied, and the sub-optimal use of new, proven, and available agrochemical technology.

The reasons for these can be traced to deficiencies in the design and implementation of water resource development programmes, and in the institutions of water governance. These arise from the conflation of authority for the development, regulation, enforcement, and conflict resolution functions in executive agencies of state governments; the fuzziness of rules governing allocations and use, and their lax enforcement; the fact that users have no role or stake in water management; the absence of any credible mechanisms for redressing grievances; the highly subsidized supply of water and energy from public systems (quite unmindful of the impact of this on the fisc, as well as the efficiency of water use); and a strong propensity of governments to exercise their authority in arbitrary ways to suit political expediency.

All these issues have had many seriously adverse consequences. Besides resulting in virtual anarchy in the management of water resources, they have induced the widespread unauthorized extraction and use of water, encouraged its wasteful and inefficient use, and given added impetus for demand to grow much faster than available supply. While water-related conflicts—and the resultant social and political tensions—have become more widespread and intense, the overexploitation of groundwater as well as the adverse impact on the ecology and environment have

also been aggravated. Attempts to address them—
through programmes for the speedier utilization
of potential, the modernization of existing systems,
greater user participation, and the restructuring of
public institutions—have been hesitant and limited to
a few states. Moreover, they have not had much of an
impact. The basic strategy of consecutive governments
has been to continue to focus on augmenting the supply of surface water and groundwater.

In order to arrest and reverse these trends, a radical
change in strategy and policy is needed. These will have
to be combined with concerted and mutually reinforcing measures to improve physical facilities, restructure
institutions, create strong inducements for the prudent
and efficient use of water, and to check the adverse
impact on sustainability. Some of the changes needed
are as follows:

- Reduce the importance given to the augmentation of supplies, and give far greater attention and
  resources to repairing and modernizing existing
  surface systems and distribution networks by equip-
  ping them with regulatory devices for better, more
  flexible regulation of water

- Reduce the fragmentation of authority and responsibility between different departments, both in the states and at the Centre
- Limit the role of the government to deciding broad objectives and priorities, and the legal framework, leaving the managerial, regulatory, and conflict resolution functions to entities autonomous of the government
- Vest all managerial functions in autonomous, user-managed organizations from the basin level down to individual systems and watersheds, without government interference, but subject to their functioning and policies being reviewed by an independent regulatory authority
- Create strong incentives for the prudent and efficient use of water by reducing the burden of implicit subsidies through a progressive and graduated increase in water and energy prices to levels that cover costs

Implementing such far-reaching reforms is, of course, difficult. The political class and the bureaucracy have strong vested interests in continuing the present regime. Users will resist any increase in water rates. Overcoming both the predictably strong opposition from all these groups as well as the practical difficulties in the way of changing a functioning regime, are daunting tasks. However, failure to confront them is no option either as it would lead to worsening of the water crisis. A calculated strategy is needed for educating all stakeholders, and strengthening ongoing efforts at reforms by extending their scope, tackling practical difficulties, and demonstrating the benefits of the reform package by implementing all its elements in select locations.

Acknowledgements

This monograph draws on the extensive Indian and global literature on water-related issues as well as my research, field studies, and knowledge gained from serving in several official committees. I have greatly benefited from the interaction and collaboration with researchers, policymakers, and water professionals in government as well as in non-governmental organizations. They are too numerous to be acknowledged individually.

However, I owe special debts to the late K.R. Datye and the late Anil Agarwal. Both were engineers by profession, and were deeply concerned about the way water resources were being exploited. The solutions they advocated emphasized the need for the discriminating use of technology, giving due importance to traditional practices, and to decentralized participatory institutions for the efficient, equitable, and sustainable use of water. Working closely with them, and the organizations they founded (Society for Promoting Participative Ecosystem Management and the Centre for Science and Environment), has shaped my own approach to research in this area. This monograph is dedicated to their memory.

I am also grateful to S. Neelakantan, Sunita Narain, and K.J. Joy for their comments and suggestions on an earlier draft, and to the editors at Oxford University Press for careful editing before publication.

Introduction

Water is critical for the sustenance of life, health, and well-being of humans, plants, and animals. The availability of water, in terms of volume and reliability, determines (a) the availability of adequate and safe water for human consumption; (b) the nature, extent, and productivity of agriculture that produces essential foods and fibre; (c) the growth of forests, grasslands, and tree crops; (d) the generation of energy, and the provision of non-agricultural products and services; and (e) the maintenance of the ecological balance and biodiversity.

The ultimate source of all freshwater on earth is rain and snowfall. Frozen ice fields in the Arctic and Antarctic regions, permanent ice in mountain glaciers elsewhere, and water stored in deep underground aquifers contain freshwater accumulated over centuries. But, relative to annual rainfall, the volume stored in them is very small. Rainfall occurs from clouds formed by moisture that evaporates from oceans, from natural or man-made water bodies that store water, from forests, crops, and all other vegetation. Of these, by far the most important part of the total evaporation is from oceans that contain 97 per cent of the earth's total stock of water. This occurs mostly during the summer season. Evapotranspiration (ET), that is, the amount of evaporation and plant transpiration from the Earth's surface to the atmosphere is also a function of temperatures: it is more in the tropics (where temperatures are higher compared to temperate climates), and in the summer as compared to rainy/winter seasons. Perennial vegetation—consisting of forests and long-duration crops—has higher rates of ET than seasonal crops. Very little evaporation occurs on uncultivated land.

The average annual precipitation over the world's land surface is approximately 836 mm, comprising 97 mm of snow and 739 mm of rainfall. About 60 per cent of this (498 mm) returns to the atmosphere due to (a) evaporation of incident rainfall from uncultivated land, exposed patches on cultivated land, and water bodies; and (b) vapour transpiration from natural and cultivated vegetation. The remaining 40 per cent emerges as water flowing in surface river systems, and as a source of replenishing groundwater aquifers.

A little more than a fourth of the rainwater flows away as subsurface runoff, and one-eighth of it emerges as surface runoff. A part of the rainwater that reaches the ground seeps through the topsoil to build up or replenish underground storages of water called aquifers. Its magnitude depends on (a) the quantum and intensity of rainfall, its distribution, and the duration of the rainy season; and (b) geological characteristics—in terms of permeability, porosity, and volume—of the aquiferous zone. This storage can be, and is, used to augment water supplies from rainfall. With advances in technology that have made it possible to tap and lift water from greater depths, the intensity of exploitation has greatly increased.

After naturally recharging moisture in the topsoil and increasing or replenishing the underground aquifers, the surplus of rainfall emerges as surface flows. Some of it fills water bodies, large and small, in natural depressions; the rest feeds streams that flow into the tributaries of major river systems. So long as they are not diverted or impounded in storages along the way, practically all the rest eventually empties into the ocean.

Before the advent of settled agriculture, the nature of vegetation and the volume of biomass produced was determined by the quantum of water available for these purposes from local rainfall and stream flows. Desert regions, with little or no rainfall, had little or no vegetation and could sustain very few, if any, living beings. In regions of higher rainfall, there is an increase in the density and productivity of natural biomass generation, with high rainfall regions being marked by dense forests and a high diversity of flora and fauna. Water needs of humans were met from local streams, natural ponds, and lakes. Nomadic pastoral communities raised large herds of domesticated animals by grazing natural pastures, often requiring seasonal migration over considerable distances. The growth of the human population beyond levels that could be sustained by hunting, gathering, and shifting cultivation led to the emergence of settled communities and the cultivation of land to produce food. Settlements tended to concentrate in areas—usually in river valleys with fertile soils and abundant and assured natural water supply—that were better placed in terms of potential crop yields.

As the population in settled areas grew, new lands in contiguous or nearby areas were brought under cultivation. However, this required clearance of forests, entailing conflict with animals, and making the land fit for cultivation almost entirely by mobilizing human labour. Areas where the scope for such expansion was large could sustain a larger population which, in turn, could muster more labour power needed for reclamation. The process of population growth and reclamation tended to go hand in hand. Further expansion was possible only by improvements in agricultural techniques and the augmentation of water supplies available from local rainfall accumulating in naturally formed lakes and ponds, by man-made devices like tanks, the diversion of water from local streams, and the use of groundwater from shallow wells.

Archaeological evidence suggests that these early developments of technology for these devices took place in many parts of the world, with more and more complex systems being devised to harness stream flows to irrigate wider areas. By the third and fourth millennium BC, such systems existed in Asia (Mesopotamia, the Indus Valley, and the Yellow River basin in north China), Egypt, and, on a more limited scale, parts of America. The techniques varied: the controlled use of flood flows in the river to irrigate dyked plots in the flood plain was characteristic of the Nile Valley; in the Euphrates/Tigris basin, river flows were used for irrigation through a combination of diversions, the drainage of marshes, and the construction of dykes and canals; flood control through the construction of massive embankments was characteristic of the method used in the Yellow River basin; while the Indus basin used a complex network of canals fed by the diversion of river flow. Archaeological evidence suggests that early American systems also used canal networks.

These were the sites of ancient civilizations that covered extensive areas with large populations and sustained prosperous, complex, and vibrant societies based on increased agricultural production made possible by irrigation. To ensure their orderly functioning, strong extra-local centres of authority and governance supported by a bureaucracy were required. These systems remained functional for centuries. In most other regions, the requirements for the basic water needs of humans and animals were met from local streams, small natural and man-made tanks and ponds, and excavated wells. Natural oases were the most valued source of water in deserts, and areas with low rainfall evolved a variety of techniques to harness rainwater to meet basic water needs and, to a limited extent, for agriculture. Some, like in the arid areas of Rajasthan, are impressively complex, both technically and in terms of institutional arrangements to manage them.

Asia has witnessed significant, though uneven, developments in technology of water control for increasing agricultural production through the first millennia BC and AD. This is manifest in the massive works to control the floods of mighty rivers of China and for diverting surface water flows in rivers and streams for irrigation through complex canal networks to sustain an extraordinarily intensive irrigated agriculture. The rise and wane of Chinese empires over the centuries is closely linked to the evolution, and vicissitudes, of its irrigation and flood control systems.

In India, the Grand Anicut that diverted Kaveri waters to irrigate extensive areas of its delta was constructed nearly 2,000 years ago. One of the largest and oldest surface systems of its kind, it still remains functional. Developments on a much smaller and more localized scale took place in India and many other Asian countries (Japan, Bali, and Sri Lanka) through the first millennium AD. The systems in Bali and Japan built elaborate, localized networks of a much smaller scale for utilizing river flow for intensive irrigation. Sri Lanka and south India pioneered techniques to impound stream flow during the monsoon in cascades of tanks. Based on sketchy data on the dates of construction of systems that have survived in our times, their number seems to have increased fitfully. But they were mostly localized and covered a relatively small proportion of total cultivated land. It is notable that, despite a chequered history punctuated by natural disasters and social and political changes, a large number continue to be functional and the tradition of management by user communities has been sustained over the centuries.

The twentieth century witnessed a phenomenal increase in water utilization the world over to meet the growing demand for water for (a) domestic use, and increasing food and fibre production for a growing, urbanizing, and prosperous population; (b) electrical energy for industries, transport and service sectors, and domestic use; and (c) industrial manufacturing processes using large volumes of processed water. This period also saw revolutionary changes in civil engineering and construction technology, and in the technology for drilling wells and lifting water with mechanical pumps from greater depths and in larger volumes.

At the turn of the century, there were relatively few large dams; by the end of the century, there were over 25,000 of them. Their storage capacity grew much faster because those constructed subsequently are larger, and the average size has been rising. In 1900, there were few dams with capacity of more than 10 mcm (million cubic metre); today nearly 3,000 have a capacity to store more than 100 mcm; 600 of them store more than a bcm (billion cubic metre); and the capacity is more than 10 bcm in some 100 of them.

The large majority of big dams have been constructed during the latter half of the twentieth century (85 per cent were commissioned after 1950). Thereafter, the rate of construction came down sharply. In 2000, the average capacity of existing dams was estimated to be around 490 mcm, and their total storage capacity over 12 tcm (trillion cubic metre).

Roughly half the dams currently registered with International Commission on Large Dams (ICOLD) are in Europe and the Americas. Both regions had an early start, and accounted for over 90 per cent of dams commissioned between 1900 and 1940; thereafter, their share fell progressively to a bare 25 per cent in the 1990s. Other regions were slower to start; but their pace picked up after the 1950s, much of it in Asia which now has over 8,000 dams (or roughly a third of the world total). Other regions have far fewer large storage.

Only 37 per cent of the world's dams are meant solely for irrigation, which means that over 60 per cent are multipurpose; 14 per cent are used for generating electricity, about one-tenth for water supply for domestic use, and 6 per cent for flood control. There are, however, striking differences in this pattern across continents.

Most dams in Asia (89 per cent) are meant to provide irrigation, with only a very small proportion being used for other purposes. In Europe, South America, and Australia, 20–30 per cent of the dams are used for power generation (compared to the world average of 14 per cent), and 13–44 per cent for water supply (the world average is 10 per cent). Irrigation as the sole use is relatively less important in North America, but it has the highest proportion of multipurpose projects as well as flood control dams.

TABLE 1 The Distribution of Large Dams across Continents by Period of Commissioning

	Pre-1900	1900–10	1920–50	1950s	1960s	1970s	1980s	1990s
Europe	350	220	700	720	1,020	1,000	820	400
Asia	50	50	200	700	1,400	2,400	2,200	1,200
North/Central America	120	400	1,400	1,000	1,800	1,600	800	220
South America	85	30	150	140	170	170	135	78
Africa	10	30	120	100	183	260	320	250
Australasia	38	40	80	60	100	100	110	40
All	630	954	2,686	2,735	4,786	5,118	4,430	2,069

Source: Pacific Institute website on 'The World's Water', available at http://www.worldwater.org/, last accessed in August 2012.

TABLE 2 Distribution of Dams across Continents by Purpose

	Irrigation	Hydro-power	Water supply	Flood control	Multi-purpose	Other	Total	Average capacity (mcm)	Total capacity (bcm)
Europe	25	31	16	3	23	2	5,480	70	38
North & Central America	11	11	10	13	30	24	8,010	998	7,994
South America	15	26	13	17	25	4	979	1,011	990
Asia	65	7	2	2	25	1	10,195	268	2,733
Africa	52	6	20	2	19	1	1,269	883	1,121
Australasia	19	19	44	1	14	3	577	205	118
All	37	14	9.4	5.9	25.4	8.5	26,510	490	12,994

Source: Pacific Institute website on 'The World's Water', available at http://www.worldwater.org/, last accessed in August 2012.

These differences reflect differences between continents in terms of the availability of surface water, the demand for water (notably, climatic conditions, size of population, the degree of urbanization), levels of income, and levels and patterns of industrialization. Some parts of the world (notably the Americas) have an abundance of uncultivated land, and are in a position to expand production by bringing more areas under cultivation. In contrast, in large parts of Asia, the scope for extending cultivated area is limited and diminishing. Yields are low because rainfall in large parts of the region is inadequate, limited to a few months, and unreliable. Increased production has to come from increased yields per unit of land. Under these conditions, the need for irrigation to increase the quantum and reliability of water supply has been critical for raising crop yields.

The twentieth century also witnessed a phenomenal expansion of groundwater extraction. Till then, shallow dug wells using manual or animal-drawn lifts were very widely used, and were the main source for meeting domestic requirements. Irrigation wells are largely concentrated in Asia, especially China and South Asia. In the early years, the use of animal power and 'Persian wheels' to lift water were the only significant techno-logical improvements. There are no statistics available on the actual number of these used or on the area irrigated. However, the magnitude of water extracted with these technologies was obviously quite limited. The picture changed dramatically with the advent of the modern technology of drilling and of mechanical pumping devices.

Though these devices came into use in developed countries early in the century, they came to Asia (which now accounts for over 80 per cent of total area irrigated by groundwater in the world) much later, and spread rapidly in only the latter half of the century. Data on worldwide trends in the number of drinking water and irrigation wells are not readily available. But it is well known that the number using mechanical pumps and tube wells has increased both in absolute terms and as a proportion of all drinking and irrigation wells. Currently, worldwide, some 113 million hectare (mha) are estimated to be irrigated by groundwater. Of this, nearly 81 mha (70 per cent) is in Asia followed by America (19 per cent). South Asia has the largest area under groundwater irrigation (48 mha); East Asia and North America each have around 19 mha.

It is insignificant in other regions (International Water Management Institute).

These developments have led to a manifold increase in total water extraction of renewable water supply from natural rainfall, dams, and groundwater. According to one widely cited estimate, the gross volume utilized in the world has increased six-and-a-half times from 579 km^3 in 1900 to 3,788 km^3 in 1995. Overall, while agricultural use has increased fivefold, non-agricultural uses have grown seventeenfold. The share of agriculture in total usage, which was close to 90 per cent at the beginning of the century, came down to about 65 per cent in 1995. The growth has been much faster in Europe (twelvefold), Americas (tenfold), and Australasia (nineteenfold), reflecting the phenomenal growth of water use for non-agricultural activities. In Asia and Africa, where the bulk of water continues to be used for agriculture, the growth is considerably smaller, and is estimated to have recorded a fivefold rise over this period.

Overall, agriculture is by far the largest user of the world's freshwater withdrawals. It has grown fivefold during the twentieth century. Usage for municipal

TABLE 3 Trends in Freshwater Withdrawal in Different
Continents (bcm)

	Total renewable supplies	1900	1940	1980	1995
Europe	6,003	37.5	96.1	449	455
North America	6,253	69.6	231	676	686
Africa	3,936	40.7	49.2	186	219
Asia	11,534	414	682	1,742	2,231
South America	13,570	15.1	32.6	117	167
Australasia	1,703	1.6	6.8	23.5	30.4
All	43,659	579	1,083	3,175	3,788

Source: Shiklomonov (1999).

areas (mostly drinking and commercial uses), and for industries, have increased much faster (eighteenfold) over this period. This reflects the impact of rapid industrialization and urbanization. The share of non-agricultural uses in total withdrawals has increased from about 13 per cent in 1900 to nearly 30 per cent by the end of the century.

It must be emphasized that these are not based on measurements of actual use but estimates based on assumptions about the relation between rainfall, surface flow, and groundwater recharge, and the growth in the volume of water used for different purposes. That actual utilization is only a fraction of total renewable supplies

TABLE 4 Trends in Worldwide Freshwater Withdrawal by End-use in the Twentieth Century (bcm)

	1900	1940	1960	1980	1995
Agriculture	513	895	1,481	2,112	2,504
Municipal areas	21.5	58.9	118	219	344
Industries	43.7	127	339	713	752
Reservoirs	0.3	4	30.2	131	108
Total	579	1,088	1,968	3,175	3,788

Source: Shiklomonov (1999).

should not be—as is often mistakenly done—taken as a measure of the potential for further expansion.

A large part of the renewable supplies is not utilizable for many reasons. A substantial amount is used by ET from forests and vegetative growth on uncultivated land, from man-made and natural impoundments of surface water; the mismatch between the spatial distribution of supplies and those of demand because of uneven distribution across seasons and regions; and serious technical, socio-economic, and political constraints that limit the extent to which these mismatches can be corrected across, and even within, countries. For instance, the renewable supply in Africa is higher than in other continents, relative to the area and to the population. Though renewable supplies are very high, they are concentrated in areas of high rainfall, with high density of forests and relatively less urbanized and prosperous economies. Water requirements for domestic use, agriculture, and non-agricultural purposes are, therefore, small relative to availability. In much of North America and Europe, temperate climates, and shorter growing seasons limit the need for irrigation. Water control to regulate and contain floods in major river basins is a more serious problem. On average, the proportion of renewable supplies that are harnessed for domestic, agricultural, and non-agricultural uses are much smaller than in the densely populated, land-scarce, and as yet less industrialized and urbanized Asia. The proportion of renewable supplies utilized in this region is higher than in other parts of the world, but is still barely 20 per cent.

The large-scale mobilization of both surface and groundwater for irrigation, flood control, and hydro-power have, until recently, been welcomed as wholly beneficial and necessary to meet the growing water requirements of a rapidly growing and increasingly prosperous population the world over. But, of late, this view has been tempered, and also contested, by the growing evidence of adverse impacts of the manner in which water resource development has been planned and managed. These include the loss of cultivated land and the large-scale displacement of existing communities; the failure to take due account of the costs of submergence of forests, and impairment of their role in preserving biodiversity; the inability to maintain minimum regime flows in rivers to keep them, and their ecosystems (including especially the coastal ecosystems) in a healthy state; inefficient and imprudent use of water resulting in the degradation of irrigated land through waterlogging and salinity; the intensification of water-related conflicts due to growing scarcity; and the overexploitation of groundwater.

These problems have grown in scale and intensity everywhere, including India. The demand for water is increasing much faster than supply. That water utilization in many regions has outstripped, or is in danger of outstripping, renewable supplies raises serious concerns about the sustainability of present trends in water consumption. Competition and conflicts between uses and users over access to available supplies have intensified and become increasingly widespread. The inability to contain and resolve water-related conflicts has led to the aggravation of social and political tensions that often spill over into violence. Current strategies for the development and management of water resources have contributed to stimulating the rapid growth of demand for human use, and have encouraged the profligate use of water with scant attention to its adverse impact in terms of land degradation, the ecological environment, and the possibility of ensuring the sustainable use of this critical and limited resource. Cumulatively, these trends—and growing evidence that they are becoming more and more widespread—have generated world-wide concern about water scarcity as a major crisis facing humanity, and the urgent need for concerted efforts on many fronts to tackle it.

1

The Indian Context

The sources of water potentially available for use in a given area consist of local rainfall, water stored in aquifers underground, water in streams and rivers flowing through its territories, and water brought from reservoirs or by diverting water flows outside its boundaries. How much is, in fact, available, or can be made available, depends on geography and geology, technology, and economic considerations. Whether or not the utilizable supplies are deemed abundant or scarce cannot be judged without considering requirements or demand.

Availability and Its Determinants

Consider a micro watershed depending entirely on rainfall. The total volume of water it can potentially harness locally is a function of its area, and the amount of rainfall it receives. A part of it is stored in the top-soil, a part seeps underground, and a part is drained out of its boundaries through streams and rivulets. Effective availability for use in the watershed consists of the amount absorbed and retained in its topsoil and underground, and impoundment or diversion of local stream flow. This depends on a host of factors besides the level of rainfall, including its seasonal distribution, the duration and intensity of rainy spells, topography, vegetation, nature and depth of soil cover, and subsurface geology.

It is apt to be low when total rainfall is low, and/or occurs mostly in a few months of the year, as also when the upper portions of the watershed are denuded, the soil cover is thin and eroded, and there is no effort to harness streams. It will be more when rainfall is higher and more evenly distributed through the year, when the upper catchments have good vegetative cover, when the soil in the lower slopes and valley are protected against erosion (by contour bunds, terracing, and appropriate land-use and cultivation practices), and measures are taken (such as construction of gully plugs, check dams, and ponds) to retain more of the local rain in small surface storages which also serve to increase groundwater recharge.

Most parts of India have relied on local rainfall for agriculture and domestic use. A variety of techniques to harness, store, and conserve local rainfall have been evolved in different parts of the country. These are embodied, for example, in the south Indian tank systems, the *ahir*s and *pyne*s of Bihar, and the many ingenious devices used in Gujarat and Rajasthan. In some areas, where terrain and rainfall permitted, water was tapped from wider catchments by constructing tanks and diverting the water flowing in the rivers. Until as recently as 1950, these were the main sources of irrigation and drinking water.

The amount of water mobilized, and the extent of area irrigated by these traditional devices was, however, constrained by the terrain, the subsurface geology, and the rainfall characteristics of each locality and its neighbourhood. A watershed with 300 mm rainfall cannot get more than this amount, even with the most effective scheme for local rainwater harvesting. The extent to which cropping intensities can be increased, and the potential for raising crop yields by using better seeds and fertilizers, therefore, depends on augmenting

3

local water supply by drawing on water resources from outside the locality. Partly for this reason, and partly because of technological developments, water resource development in recent times has tended to concentrate on large storage-based irrigation, and pumping underground water from greater depths.

In India, typically, the upper catchments of river basins are characterized by relatively high rainfall, mountainous terrain, and low population density. The potential for use in local agriculture and the requirements for human consumption (being conditioned by topography and human settlement patterns) on the other hand, are rather limited in relation to local water resources. By contrast, the current and prospective need for water for agricultural, domestic, and even industrial uses in the plains and lower reaches is larger, often much larger, than local resources. They tend to have lower and less reliable rainfall, are more densely populated, and much of the agricultural activity and the potential for expanding it is concentrated in them. This mismatch permits the manipulation of surface flows through storage or diversion to make more water available to segments of the basin where the needs and potentials for use are much higher than the supply from local precipitation.

The possibilities in this respect have greatly expanded because of advances in techniques of construction of reservoirs, transport, and the regulation of water distribution through extensive canal networks over long distances, and for lifting groundwater. The latter half of the twentieth century in India has witnessed phenomenal growth in the volume of water stored in large surface storages, and pumped from underground sources. Massive resources have gone into the harnessing of river flows by constructing large reservoir-based canal systems under the auspices of the government. Groundwater exploitation, though largely in the private sector, has been actively encouraged and facilitated by the government.

Renewable Supplies

With a total area of some 3.3 million km, India receives, on average, 1,100 mm of rainfall a year. The total volume of rainfall in the country is around 4,000 bcm. Together with inflows from outside its borders (estimated at 600 bcm), it gets on average 4,600 bcm of water a year. All of this is not available for use within the country. A large part goes back into the atmosphere through evaporation soon after it reaches the ground and, subsequently, from land without any vegetative cover, from pastures and other vegetation growing naturally on uncultivated land, from rivers, streams, storages and other water bodies, and from bare patches of cultivated land. These are not amenable to control. Another large part (estimated at 1,200 bcm) flows out of the country to other countries in fulfilment of obligations under water-sharing treaties, and because the unutilized—and unutilizable—flows through domestic rivers drain into the sea.

The proportion of renewable water generated from internal rainfall is relatively low compared to relatively large and densely populated countries. India has higher temperatures throughout the year as well as moderately high precipitation, but is marked by greater seasonal concentration. Natural evaporation from various sources being relatively high, renewable supplies as a proportion of total precipitation are low.

The current official assessment is that the internally generated supply of surface water (in a normal year)

TABLE 5 Temperatures and Rainfall in Select Countries across Continents and Climatic Conditions

	Temperature*		Rainfall (mm)					Wet	cloud
	Mean	Max	Total	MAM	JJA	SON	DJF	days	days
India	23.7	29.6	1,083	104	669	270	40	54	40
China	6.9	15	627	146	313	126	42	108	54
Indonesia	25.8	30.6	2,702	772	516	613	802	203	64
South Korea	11.8	16.5	1,404	287	723	283	111	120	53
Thailand	26.3	31.4	1,622	331	631	531	80	137	60
Egypt	22.1	29.4	51	13	8	9	20	9	28
South Africa	17.8	24.9	495	124	53	124	193	70	35
USA	8.5	14.9	736	182	207	184	162	105	59
Canada	-5.4		537	101	182	149	104	128	62
Mexico	21	28.5	752	73	367	243	68	63	53
Brazil	24.9	30.3	1,752	564	214	358	647	211	71
France	10.7	15	867	217	186	236	228	164	63
Spain	13.3	18.7	636	171	86	183	197	123	52
Australia	21.6		535	142	74	33	236	64	38

Source: Tyndall Centre for Climatic Research, available at http://www.cru.uea.ac.uk, accessed in August 2012.
Note: * In degrees centigrade; MAM refers to March–April–May; JJA refers to June–July–August; SON refers to September–October–November; and DJF refers to December–January–February.

is around 1,200 bcm, and the groundwater potential is around 420 bcm. Allowing for overlap between the two sources, the net usable supplies available internally are placed at 1,230 bcm. Taken together with the 600 bcm of externally generated surface flows, total renewable supplies are estimated to be 1,830 bcm. It must be noted that these estimates refer to rainfall and renewable supplies on average over a relatively long period. All these are subject to significant variations from year to year due to vagaries of rainfall.

Nearly a fourth of the country's districts face the prospect of a moderate drought (actual rainfall falling below 25 per cent of normal in any given year), and about one in 12 face the prospect of a severe drought (actual precipitation being less than half of the normal). Nearly 75 per cent of the annual rainfall occurs between June and September, most of it in 54 days, and concentrated in about 100 hours.

During the monsoon, temperatures and natural evaporation rates are much lower than precipitation. As a result, the bulk of the renewable supplies occur during this period. Rainfall during the post-monsoon season is much lower, as are the extent of cultivation and the contribution of rainfall to renewable supplies because evaporation rates are much higher than rainfall. Rivers and streams decline to negligible levels in non-perennial rivers, and fall sharply even in perennial rivers in summer, when rainfall is scanty and soils are everywhere too parched to sustain vegetative growth.

In all these respects, there are large regional variations. The Indus, Ganges, and Brahmaputra basins, which receive roughly two-fifths of the total rainfall, account for over 60 per cent of the renewable freshwater supplies. This is largely because all three basins get large inflows from outside the borders; and, in the case of the Brahmaputra, because of the very high rainfall in its catchment areas. In all other basins, the average precipitation is lower and marked by wide variation. Thus, their contribution to renewable supplies is much less, but in varying degrees, than their share in total rainfall.

Large parts of the east-flowing rivers of the Peninsula (Godavari, Krishna, Kaveri) have relatively low rainfall, but benefit from the high rainfall in the Western Ghats. They account for about a sixth of the rainfall and about one-eighth of renewable supply. The catchments of east-flowing rivers originating in the central Indian plateau (Brahmani, Baitarni, Subarnarekha, Mahanadi, and some smaller rivers to its south) have 10 per cent of the country's total rainfall and account for about 7 per cent of renewable supplies. West-flowing rivers of central India (Narmada and Tapti), whose catchment receives about 10 per cent of the country's total rainfall, are estimated to generate 7 per cent of renewable flows. The western coastal region, where rainfall is well above the national average, is notable in that its share in renewable supplies (over 10 per cent) is much higher than its share in total rainfall (6 per cent).

Utilizable Resources

Not all the renewable supply is, however, utilizable. The current official estimate places the potentially usable water resources at 1,032 bcm, consisting of 690 bcm from surface sources and 342 bcm of groundwater. It is noteworthy that, except in the Gangetic plains and Brahmaputra, official assessment implies that the entire renewable supplies are utilizable. Most of the resources considered be unutilizable are concentrated in the Brahmaputra (500 bcm), Ganges (100 bcm), and rivers of the western coast (150 bcm).

TABLE 6 The Distribution of Precipitation, and Renewable and Utilizable Supplies of Water in India

	Basin area 000 km²	Total precipitation (bcm)	Renewable supplies (bcm)	Utilizable flow (bcm)
Indus, Ganges, Brahmaputra	1,200	1,476	1,183	550
East-flowing south of Ganges to Godavari	310	390	130	119
East-flowing peninsular rivers	750	660	230	250
West-flowing rivers of central India	220	225	75	80
West-flowing along the west coast	112	321	200	54
Saurashtra–Kutch	321		15	26
All	2,910	3,072	1,833	1,079

Source: Central Water Commission, Government of India.

The volume of water flowing through the Brahmaputra is simply too massive to be harnessed. The scope for using it for irrigation is limited by geography. The problem here is one of flood control—a task that has proved unmanageable. The idea of constructing dams in upper catchments to store water for hydropower generation has been advocated, and is being currently pursued. There are serious concerns about the risks involved in constructing dams—some of which are of huge dimensions—in a region prone to high seismic activity. The environmental damage that an earthquake could cause is also a matter of widespread concern.

Similar considerations limit the utilizable volume in the Ganges basin: many of the potential storages are in the seismic zone, and developments are contingent on forging agreements with Nepal. Moreover, India has obligations to ensure that a portion of the surface flows is made available to Bangladesh. The Gangetic plains are rich in groundwater; but there are no systematic and objective assessments of the extent to which the potential has been exploited, and how much more may be available. Utilizable flows in the rivers of the western coast are low because of the lack of sites for storing them, and the limited need and scope for using stored water for irrigation.

The magnitude of surface systems, and the magnitude and duration for which they can augment local rainfall, depends on the size of their catchments and the characteristics of rainfall. Systems drawing their supplies from small catchments with low rainfall tend to be small in size. The extent to which they can supplement rainfall also tends to be limited, and more volatile. This is typically the case with small local systems. Large reservoirs draw their supplies from larger catchments, and can tap precipitation in higher rainfall areas, further away from their commands. Catchments with larger, and more evenly distributed, rainfall can provide larger quantities of more assured and less volatile supplies which can be used over a longer period of the year. Inter-year variability of rainfall in catchments also results in variability in water inflows into reservoirs. Its impact, again, is a function of the size of catchments.

The rate of natural groundwater recharge is also influenced by the quantum and seasonal concentration of rainfall, terrain, and subsurface geology. It is low in areas of low rainfall (Indus plains, western Rajasthan,

Saurashtra, and Kutch), in hilly terrains (upper catchments of river basins), regions with heavy soils (black cotton soils of the Deccan), and in hard-rock regions (much of the Deccan Plateau). In large parts of central India, the recharge potential is low even with moderate rainfall due to the combination of the relatively shallow cover of permeable soils, the uneven terrain, and unfavourable geology. Recharge tends to be concentrated in pockets, especially valley bottoms, where conditions are more favourable. Conditions for natural recharge are also not favourable in the plains of Bengal, coastal Odisha, and the Brahmaputra Valley which have excessive rainfall, and are prone to floods.

The potential for recharge is most favourable in the alluvial plains of northern India, which have extensive areas of deep soils that can absorb and store huge quantities of water underground. Natural recharge under these conditions is largely a function of rainfall. In all these tracts, substantial recharge occurs in the command of surface systems. This is particularly striking in the Punjab, Haryana, and north Rajasthan where canals irrigate a high proportion of cultivated land. Since groundwater can be stored with minimal loss and leakage compared to surface water, the variability in rainfall is less likely to impact on the availability of groundwater in areas of high natural recharge potential, and especially in areas where the groundwater storage capacity is high.

The need for irrigation also varies with agro-climatic conditions. Water requirements of natural forests, cultivated seasonal food and fibre crops, and perennial tree crops grown under rainfed conditions, are met entirely by rainfall. Forests are generally concentrated in higher elevations whose hilly terrain does not permit much cultivation, and where rainfall is generally higher than in the lowlands. But their characteristics and productivity are conditioned by the level, seasonal distribution, and reliability of rainfall. The density of forest cover tends to be greater in regions with higher rainfall than under low rainfall regimes. Species compositions, and the volume of biomass they produce, also vary with rainfall and elevation.

The quantum, seasonal patterns, and the reliability of rainfall determine when and what kinds of crops can be grown as well as the attainable level of yields under unirrigated conditions. With the onset of the rains, all forms of natural vegetation revive. In most parts of the country, the main cropping season for rain-fed agriculture is during the southwest monsoon; in other areas (mostly parts of the south and east India) it is during October to December. The quantum, timing, and intensity of rainfall during the season relative to the water required for healthy crop growth (also a function of temperatures) are all variable across regions, and from year to year. In some parts of the country (notably the Saurashtra–Kutch regions of Gujarat, western Rajasthan, and Punjab-Haryana), the total rainfall in the season is less than evapotranspiration (ET).

Over a large part of the rest of the country, precipitation volumes are close to that of ET in the monsoon season. Uncertainty about timing and the quantum of rain in these tracts makes for considerable volatility in both areas and yields. Their relative magnitudes are a crucial determinant of cropping patterns. Under these conditions, the main crops are sorghum, millets, pulses, oilseeds, cotton, and others which need less water in combinations that are adapted to varying local conditions. The possibility of raising yields by using improved biochemical technology that calls for larger and more dependable water is also severely constrained. Not surprisingly, the productivity of rainfed lands is low, prone to large fluctuations, and with limited scope for improvement.

Those areas (notably in Assam, the eastern parts of the Gangetic Plain, coastal Odisha, and the west coast) with rainfall substantially more than ET in the kharif season, tend to grow paddy and some water-intensive seasonal crops. Large parts of the present-day Brahmaputra basin and lower Gangetic plains are prone to heavy flooding by overflowing rivers during the monsoon. In these regions, until recently, no massive flood control works were undertaken; instead, the fertile silt that was left behind by the floods provided the basis for raising crops. While the productivity of land is much higher and more assured than in low rainfall regions, weather-induced volatility in production and the scope for raising yields by adopting improved biochemical technology that call for careful water management remains a problem. By collecting local rainfall in local tanks and ponds, tapping water flowing in nearby streams, and/or extracting groundwater from shallow wells, it is possible to take care of inadequate soil moisture during dry spells within the main cropping season. However, the scope for these devices is limited by the magnitude of local rainfall and the terrain.

Growing crops that need more water than is available from local sources, or take a longer time to mature, is possible only if local supplies are augmented substantially by tapping water from streams and rivers that are fed from wider catchments, or by increasing groundwater extraction. The extent to which this is possible is, however, constrained by technology, the capacity to mobilize resources which can exploit these possibilities, and the creation of organizations capable of managing them.

2

Evolution of Water Control

For the most part, early attempts at augmenting limited supplies of water from rainfall were confined to small-scale works to tap local sources. Ancient scriptures and secular literature—most of which are dated long after the disappearance of the Indus Valley civilization—refer to the construction and improvement of water control works as activities beneficial to people's welfare, and deserving to be supported and promoted by kings. Apart from the Grand Anicut, most of these were small-scale storages to complement local rainfall and were made up of water diverted from local streams and shallow dug wells, undertaken locally by large landowners, regional chieftains, and temples. Some of these extant works—such as the ahirs and pynes of

Bihar, the water-harvesting systems of Rajasthan, and the tanks of south India—have survived, and remained functional for many centuries. They are living witnesses to the significant innovations that must have gone into developing techniques and institutions adapted to varied physical, climatic, and social conditions. Through modern times, these works, though limited in the volume of water they tapped, were widely distributed and served as the main source of water for domestic use and for irrigation in most communities.

Our knowledge of the historical evolution of such innovations is quite scanty. But from all available evidence, these works grew fitfully, and at a relatively slow pace, well into the first millennium CE. Their impact on agriculture is likely to have been localized to areas with relatively more rainfall, to communities favourably situated in terms of proximity to streams and rivers, and in areas where the terrain was conducive to the construction of tanks and ponds. The notion that rulers should support and encourage such works as a means of promoting the welfare of citizens, and as a means of garnering revenues to strengthen their power and expand their territorial domains, has been supported from Vedic times. Governments began to play a more active role in encouraging the proper maintenance of such works, and constructing more of them (especially those calling for larger outlays and more complex organizations) in periods of stability, and in restoring damages caused by intermittent wars and military conflicts.

Data regarding the number and kinds of such works are also inadequate. Tanks are largely concentrated in peninsular India, and diversions for tapping stream flow are more prominent in central India, Bihar, Odisha, and other hilly regions. Most were managed by local communities. By all accounts, till medieval times, the state did not devote much attention or resources to existing works, and much less to improving them, or constructing large new ones. In the north, canals to divert the waters of the Yamuna for irrigation of large areas were constructed by the Tughlaks and, subsequently, by Mughal rulers during the thirteenth to fifteenth centuries. The Vijayanagara kings and the rulers of the Deccan in the fifteenth century also extended surface irrigation through canals and tanks in the south. These, and subsequent periods, witnessed greater interest among rulers in expanding and improving irrigation for increasing agricultural production which would not only benefit citizens, but also provide larger, more secure revenues for the exchequer.

Many of the same considerations led governments in the early phases of the colonial era to take active interest in the renovation and improvement of existing irrigation works. Besides expanding the irrigation network of the Kaveri delta, many large-scale surface irrigation works were taken up in the middle of the nineteenth century. These include the Upper Ganga Canal, the Upper Bari Doab Canal, and the Krishna and the Godavari delta systems. All these have anicuts built across the rivers to divert flow through canal networks for irrigating extensive areas. They incorporated many innovations in design and construction technology which were acclaimed as pioneering contributions at the time. However, in the process, most of the limited numbers of sites suitable for diversion works were exploited. It was also realized that the construction of storages to store surplus monsoon flows, and canal systems to transport the water over long distances would be necessary, both for protecting regions with low rainfall against recurrent droughts and famine, and for enabling regions wholly dependent on seasonal rainfall to make more intensive and productive use of land.

Some visionary engineers—of whom Arthur Cotton is the most famous—recognized that construction of large storages would be needed to compound surplus flows during the monsoon, and the potential it would open up for increasing production and raising crops during season. The feasibility of constructing such storages was demonstrated by works undertaken in the USA and Europe. Such works involved the mobilization of financial resources and the creation of organizations on a scale that only governments could manage. Cotton undertook an extensive survey of potential storage sites on many major rivers of the country.

Technological developments gradually made it possible to construct large storages and canal systems which required large resources to construct and a professional bureaucracy to manage them. The notion of the State's right of 'eminent domain' and the absolute ownership of all rivers took root, and provided the legal basis for the government to assume the exclusive power and responsibility of developing surface water resources, as well as to impose restrictions on individuals, communities, and the private sector from accessing and using water flowing in rivers and streams without the explicit approval of the government. Pre-existing small local works were largely left to be managed by individuals and local institutions in the traditional manner. The power to construct and manage new projects of this kind was also taken over by the state. Specialized agencies were set up by the government for planning new projects, organizing their construction, maintaining the physical structures in good repair, and regulating the distribution of water between different uses and users served by them. These agencies (generally a part of public works departments and, in some cases, specifically for irrigation works) were manned by professional engineers and trained technical field staff to undertake preparatory surveys, design, construct, and manage the projects.

Both resource constraints and concerns about the prospect of recovering costs led colonial governments to adopt a cautious policy before undertaking such projects. Pressure for state funding of such works to protect farmers against droughts and famines resulted in some works being undertaken on these grounds. However, this was done reluctantly and on a limited scale because adequate revenues could not be generated, and the state exchequer could not bear large and continuing losses. The government, therefore, decided that it would undertake investment in irrigation projects only if additional revenues generated by way of land revenue and water charges from beneficiary farmers would be large enough to meet the costs of maintaining and operating them and leave a surplus to provide a minimum rate of return on the capital invested. In many cases, the government insisted on potential beneficiaries contributing a part of the investment costs as a condition for committing state funds for implementing the project.

The late nineteenth and the first half of the twentieth centuries saw many such projects being built on this basis. Dams like Krishna Raja Sagara and Mettur were constructed across the Kaveri river during this period. Storages were identified on the Tungabhadra, Krishna, Narmada, Sabarmati, Mahi, and Sutlej rivers. Though unprecedented when compared to what was done during the previous two centuries, the scale and pace of their contribution to the expansion of irrigated areas was quite modest. The acute food shortages and the Bengal Famine during World War II led the government to decide that the development of irrigation would be an important part of the post-war reconstruction programme.

In 1945, the Government of India set up the Central Waterways, Irrigation and Navigation Commission (CWINC) to conduct surveys and investigations for the planned utilization of water resources of the country as a whole, and to implement schemes for the conservation, control, and regulation of water and waterways, in consultation with provincial governments. The Commission conducted detailed surveys, investigations, and designs of many large-scale projects, with Hirakud, Bhakra Nangal, and Tungabhadra being among the more prominent. Work on some of them started even before Independence.

Post-Independence Developments

After Independence, the development of water resources on a large-scale to meet basic needs and to extend irrigation for raising food production became a key element in the strategy for agricultural development. Under the Constitution of independent India, water resource development and management was designated as a state subject. However, the states were required to get the Centre's approval and clearance for projects on interstate rivers. The Centre was also given the authority to devise mechanisms for deciding the allocation of waters in rivers between riparian states, and for the settlement of disputes relating to it. With the advent of planning, the government assumed direct responsibility to undertake and manage water resource projects for irrigation, power generation, and flood control, as well as non-agricultural uses and to finance the cost of their development from public funds.

Initially, plans provided for implementation of many ongoing and new large-scale projects for irrigation, power generation, and flood control; for improvement of existing minor irrigation works, and construction of new ones. Plans also made modest provisions for programmes augmenting drinking water supply. While the larger projects were subject to clearance by the Planning Commission, minor irrigation works and water supply schemes were largely left to be planned, implemented, and monitored by the states.

The scale of direct outlays on all irrigation components increased rapidly in successive plans, but their composition changed decisively in favour of large-scale surface works. While the bulk of the allocations for this sector was for new projects, substantial amounts were spent on schemes for the development of command areas to enable the speedy utilization of the potential created and, more recently, for the rehabilitation and modernization of old systems. Increases in allocations for direct investment in minor surface irrigation works were much smaller, and were phased out over time. Between 1951 and 2010, the public sector has spent close to Rs 3,870 billion on irrigation and flood-control programmes. More than three-fourths of it has gone into major and medium projects; and a little under one-fifth to minor irrigation; flood control accounts for about 3 per cent of the total. This has led to a widespread and manifold expansion in irrigation facilities using surface water.

Large-scale Surface Storages

At the time of Independence, the country had 300 large dams. Currently, there are 4,700 completed dams, and another 500 are under construction. The large majority (70 per cent) of them were completed during the 1970s and 1980s. Newer dams were larger: the average storage capacity per dam increased from 35 mcm in 1951 to 54 mcm. The live storage capacity varies from 10 million cubic metres (mcm) to 9 billion cubic metres (bcm). The capacity of 98 per cent of the dams is less than 100 mcm with an average capacity of about 20 mcm. Their total capacity (83 bcm) accounts for a little less than 40 per cent of the capacity of all dams. Dams with capacity of more than 100 mcm comprise less than 2 per cent of the total in terms of numbers but account for 60 per cent of total storage capacity.

TABLE 7   Number and Storage Capacity of Large Dams of Different Sizes

	<0.1 bcm	0.1–0.5 bcm	0.5–1 bcm	1.0–2.5 bcm	2.5–5 bcm	5 bcm	All
Number	3,974	21	21	15	10	8	4,052
Capacity (bcm)	83	4.8	16	25.2	32.4	52.6	214

Source: CWC, *Water and Related Statistics* (2007).
Note: Estimates relate to 2001.

Most reservoirs are meant primarily for irrigation; but several (especially large ones) are designed for multiple purposes, including irrigation, flood control, and the generation of electricity. Requirements for domestic, industrial, and other non-agricultural purposes were met partly from these reservoirs. Some were dedicated wholly for these purposes. Between 1951 and 2000, the live storage capacity of large dams is reported to have increased from 12.5 bcm to 214 bcm, and the volume of water supplied by major and medium irrigation systems is estimated to have increased more than fivefold: from 90 bcm to 520 bcm. Currently (2007), major and medium works are estimated to have the potential to irrigate 47 mha of crop area in a year; the actual utilization is placed at 37 mha.

Minor Surface Irrigation Works

Plan documents give little information about the distribution of outlays on minor surface irrigation, on the repair and rehabilitation of existing schemes, the construction of new works, the net addition to the number of works of different categories, or the quantum of water that they provide for various uses. There is a widespread impression that many of the older works have deteriorated due to neglect and have become derelict; and the capacity of many more to deliver water has declined. Official land-use statistics, in fact, do show a progressive decline in area irrigated by these sources: from around 6 mha to 7 mha in the early 1950s to around 3 mha currently.

However, a recent (2001) census of all minor irrigation (MI) works shows that the number of these works, and the area they irrigate, is much larger than the above data suggest. There are 1.2 million small-scale irrigation works in the country using surface water. Roughly half of them draw water from tanks, other storages, and the diversion of local streams. The other half use water lifted from rivers, streams, canals, and tanks. About two-fifths of storage/diversion works have been set up by the government, and a little over a third are owned by individual farmers. About 15 per cent of the works enumerated were not in use. The average area irrigated per work in these categories is barely 10 ha. There are tanks and permanent diversions that irrigate much larger areas: over a hundred ha in several cases and as much as 5,000 ha in a few. Most, however, serve less than 10 ha. It must be noted that water from these works is used for both agricultural and non-agricultural uses. In fact, until recently, they have been the main source for meeting basic water needs of several hundred thousand rural communities, as well as numerous urban centres.

Lifting water from streams, rivers, and canals is a relatively recent phenomenon. It has spread rapidly because of the strong demand for irrigation, the advent of energized pumps, an ambivalent law regarding the

TABLE 8 Characteristics of Minor Surface Irrigation Works, 2000

	Surface minor irrigation				Minor irrigation; lift		
Type	Number in use 000' ha	Potential mha	Utilization mha	Type	Number in use 000' ha	Potential mha	Utilization mha
Tanks	233	3.6	2.3	On river	289	1.78	1.19
Other streams	120	1.33	0.92	On stream	98.6	0.43	0.33
Permanent diversions	69	1.4	1.13	On main canal	63	0.4	0.27
Temporary diversions	90	0.68	0.51	On tank	118	0.36	0.22
Conservation—	27	0.39	0.14				
Groundwater schemes							
All	539	7.4	5.0	All	563	2.95	2

Source: Government of India (2005).

lifting of water from rivers and canals, and the lax attitude of the government to regulating it. Most surface lifts use energized pumps, and are owned by individual farmers. On an average, works in this category irrigate around 4 ha. Nearly 90 per cent of surface lift works are reported to be in use.

The census also shows that a substantial number of works in both categories are of relatively recent origin. About 15 per cent of the 640 thousand surface storage and diversion schemes are reported to have been set up during the 1990s. The comparable proportion for surface lifts is much higher: at about a third of the total number. The general impression that minor irrigation works have been stagnant, or even declining, is clearly questionable. The number of works (and possibly their contribution as a source of water for a variety of local uses) is evidently growing. Moreover, much of this growth has come from private investment. The characteristics of this growth and their underlying factors call for closer study.

According to the MI census, works in this category have the potential to irrigate 10.4 mha of crop area, and the area actually irrigated is placed at around

7 mha. These figures are substantially higher than the estimates reported in plan documents.

The MI censuses have shown that

- they are more numerous, diverse, and widely diffused than is generally believed;
- they are growing, both in numbers and in terms of area irrigated;
- surface flow and surface lift schemes are roughly equal in numbers, but flow schemes are, on an average, much bigger, and account for nearly 70 per cent of potential;
- nearly half the surface schemes, and 90 per cent of lift schemes, are owned and operated by farmers, individually or collectively;
- only a small proportion is located within the command of major and medium projects;
- most schemes are in use, but only 60 per cent of the potential was being utilized during the survey year; and
- the major portion of crop area irrigated by this source is in the *kharif* season, and about 30 per cent in the rabi season.

The census has not collected much information on works that have been abandoned, become derelict, or been encroached upon. Nor do they give any information on how public systems (mostly tanks and storages) are managed. Based on official reports and the findings of surveys by researchers in south India, which has the largest number of tanks, the following features stand out:

- More and more tanks located in and around growing cities and towns have gone out of use as tank beds, and are increasingly encroached upon, or being used for housing and commercial purposes, or their water has become polluted due to the dumping of garbage and sewage.
- The silting of tank beds, the encroachment of foreshore areas, and the damaged condition of bunds, sluices, and surplus weirs is common. The extent and severity varies; but in most cases (at least in Tamil Nadu), this does not seem to have resulted in any reduction in the effective ayacut.
- In general, governments (or panchayats) have taken the responsibility for the repair and maintenance of

tanks above a certain size. In some states (for instance, Andhra Pradesh and Karnataka), the regulation of water supply for irrigation is also entrusted to government functionaries. In other states (notably Tamil Nadu), traditional but informal village institutions play an active role, both in the maintenance of the distribution network and the regulation of water supply. Smaller public tanks are left to be managed by local communities.

- Extensive surveys in Tamil Nadu show that these local institutions function according to the rules and conventions regarding the timing of the release of water, the regulation of water supply to different segments of the command, the participation of users in maintenance both when supply to the tank is normal and when there are shortages. There are also mechanisms and procedures for settling disputes. There are also conventions that recognize the rights of the village as a whole to the usufruct of trees and other biomass growing on bunds, as also the fish in the tanks.

- In the past, the smooth functioning of these institutions depended on the existence of strong centres of social authority and power in villages. Usually, large landowning families from dominant castes played a key role in ensuring that these conventions and rules were observed. An important reason for this is that since tank water is a common pool resource, and the livelihood of users depended crucially on its orderly management, users had strong common interests and incentives to observe rules and conventions. The process was far from smooth or fair to all sections of users. Nevertheless, many old tanks have remained functional for long periods, often centuries.

- However, local institutions have been changing for many reasons: the proliferation of the number of users; the diffusion of landownership across social groups; and the declining power of the dominant castes. This has increased the potential for conflict among users, and has also made the task of enforcing rules, and resolving disputes, more difficult.

- With the spread of wells in the ayacut, and the reduced dependence of well owners on tank water, this shared interest and, therefore, the functioning of institutions of collective action weakened. However, this did not lead everywhere to their collapse. With regard to most tanks surveyed, while the institutions for tank management have become looser, they continue to function in a more or less orderly fashion.

Groundwater

Direct public investment in groundwater development is negligible. For a brief period in the 1950s, the government tried to use newly developing technology for extracting water through public tube wells. A sizeable number of them were drilled—mostly in UP—to supply irrigation water to farmers. But this was soon given up because of difficulties in management, widespread complaints of inefficient operation, and the fact that they were incurring huge losses. The public tube well programme for irrigation was phased out, and the emphasis shifted to encouraging private investment by providing financial assistance through public institutions and various other incentives. The regulation of groundwater use and policies for the pricing of electricity has been left entirely to the states.

The use of groundwater has grown apace. In the early 1950s, only dug wells were used to extract groundwater for irrigation and domestic use. Almost all of them were of shallow depth. Water was lifted manually or by using animal power. Persian wheels, also driven by animals, were widely used in north India. In some areas mechanically operated pumps were introduced earlier. Though pump technology made it possible to lift larger volumes of water from greater depths, their use was very limited, because the infrastructure for supplying the energy to operate them was yet to develop. This constraint was eased with the rural electrification programme taken up as part of the strategy of agricultural development. As this grew, farmers' interest in excavating new wells and installing energized pumps also increased. Since the mid–1960s, the government has adopted a more proactive policy of encouraging and facilitating groundwater development by farmers.

The use of electrical pumps made it possible to pump larger volumes of water per unit of time, and also tap water from greater depths. This, of course, called for larger investments; but higher costs were more than met by the increased production that they made possible. Private wells have given farmers greater control in regulating the timing and quantum of irrigation according to actual crop conditions—with smaller losses and waste—than was possible with uncertain canal supplies. The returns to investment in wells, tube wells, and pumps have also increased with new seed-fertilizer technology greatly increasing productivity per unit of water, reinforced by the policy of subsidizing electricity for farmers. Moreover, restrictions on the construction and deepening of wells, and conditions for getting power connections, were relaxed and a larger supply of credit for such investments was made available at relatively low interest through cooperatives.

The cumulative impact has led to a rapid expansion in the number of open wells, and the use of energized pumps. The number of open wells used for irrigation increased from 3.9 million in 1951 to 6.1 million in 1968, and 10 million in 1994. Their numbers have remained more or less at the same level in 2001. The proportion of energized wells, which was negligible in 1951, has increased progressively to around 20 per cent in 1968, 70 per cent in 1994, and 80 per cent in 2001. Wells have become deeper, and tend to use more powerful pumps.

Even more phenomenal is the growth in the number of private tube wells, all of which necessarily have to use mechanical pumps of a higher horsepower. The number of tube wells, which was less than 0.5 million in 1968, exceeded 5 million in 1994, and touched

9 million in 2000. Currently, most (8.4 million) of these are shallow tube wells. Deep tube wells have grown rapidly, and their number in 2000 is placed at a little over a half a million.

TABLE 9 Growth of Groundwater Irrigation, 1951–94

	1951★	1968★	1994@	2001@
Open wells No 10^6	3.9	6.1	10.2	9.6
Energized 10^6	Neg	1.4	7.2	8.2
Net area irrigated 10^6 ha	6.0	8.0	12.4	13.2
Tube wells No 10^6	Neg	0.4	5.1	8.8
Energized 10^6	Neg	0.4	5.1	8.2
Net area irrigated 10^6 ha	Neg	4.5	18.4	31.8

Source: ★Central Water Commission and @Government of India (2005).

Irrigation wells have been and are still used as a source of water for domestic use and for animal care in rural areas. There has also been a huge expansion in the number of wells and tube wells—mostly in the private sector but also to feed public water supply systems—to meet the growing demand for non-agricultural uses. But little is known about their number or the volume of water they supply.

According to Planning Commission estimates, the irrigation potential of wells and tube wells has increased from a little over 8 mha of crop area in 1961, to 43 mha in 2001–2; actual utilization has grown much slower, and is placed at 39 mha in 2001. These estimates are much lower than those of the MI census which placed the total irrigation potential of wells and tube wells in 2000 at 58 mha, and the area actually irrigated at 45 mha.

Most of the investment in groundwater development has been in the private sector. Investment has gone not only into the increasing the number of wells, tube wells, and pump sets, but also into the deepening of existing wells and the installation of more powerful pumps to cope with declining water tables. Estimates of the magnitude, composition, and mode of financing of this investment are not available However, with declining water tables and rising costs, the volume of water extracted by them has not increased in the same proportion as investments.

Water Utilization by Source and Use

Available data on the volume of water utilized from different man-made sources and for different uses are inadequate in terms of coverage, detail and reliability. There are no measurements of the total and source-wise volume of water actually supplied for different uses. Published estimates for surface water relate only to major river basins at a few points in time. There are no estimates for minor surface works. Groundwater estimates are based on norms of water extraction for different kinds of wells in different regions. The following figures must, therefore, be treated as very rough estimates.

The total volume of water utilization from all surface works and groundwater is estimated to have increased from around 170–80 bcm in the early 1950s to 630 bcm in 2000. Utilization from surface works is estimated to have increased from around 115 bcm in the early 1950s to around 520 bcm at the turn of the century, and that of groundwater from 40 bcm to around 110 bcm. Over the same period, the volume utilized from irrigation works is estimated to have grown from 155 bcm per year to 550 bcm in 2000. The rest is presumed to be used for non-agricultural purposes. Details of the use of irrigation water and its impact on agricultural productivity are discussed at length in the subsequent sections. But the estimates for non-agricultural uses and its effectiveness need to be used with great circumspection.

Non-agricultural needs for water have, of course, been increasing. In the 1950s, most of the requirement for domestic consumption was met from local sources, mainly groundwater. The requirements for other non-agricultural uses were also quite limited. With growing urbanization and industrialization, non-agricultural demand has grown more rapidly than that of agriculture. But little is known about the magnitudes of consumption for different non-agricultural uses, and the sources from which they are met.

Water from reservoirs, canals, and wells is used mostly, but not exclusively, for agriculture. It is also used for domestic and non-agricultural uses by habitations in their neighbourhood. In many cases, non-agricultural requirements of urban areas are met from water available in surface irrigation systems. Their extent is not known; but it is believed to be comparatively small relative to the requirements.

The government has taken up projects specifically meant to provide safe and assured water supply for domestic use in rural and urban areas, and to meet the growing demand for non-agricultural uses. A large—and probably increasing—part of their needs are being met from private groundwater sources and from public irrigation systems. However, there is hardly any data on either the overall magnitude of the actual usage for different purposes or of the relative contributions of different sources even at the national level.

Outlays on public sector schemes for rural and urban water supply have grown manifold. The total outlay on these programmes up to the end of the Tenth Plan is over Rs 1,000 billion (about 70 per cent of it on rural and 30 per cent on urban areas). Outlays during the Eleventh Plan are placed at one-and-a-half times this figure, bringing the total to more than Rs 2,500 billion. There is, however, no credible independent assessment of their impact in terms of the effective increase in coverage, and of actual water use.

According to official estimates, the proportion of villages with access to protected sources of drinking water has increased from 56 per cent in 1991 to nearly three-fourths in 2007. The reported coverage in urban centres is much higher, and is currently placed at over 90 per cent. Coverage is, however, a rather vague concept. A better indicator is the proportion of households that depend on wells and other traditional sources that are usually considered unsafe. According to the 2001 census, more than a fourth of the rural households depend on open wells and other traditional sources considered unsafe; but about half the households have access to hand pumps and tube wells; and about a fourth have a tap. Moreover, only 30 per cent of rural households have access to a water source on their premises. The situation, in all these respects, is much better in urban areas where more than two-thirds of households report having access to piped supply. Less than 10 per cent depend on wells and traditional sources; most report having access to a water source on their premises.

There is no information on either the quantity or quality of water actually used by rural households from different sources. In urban areas, most metropolitan towns are covered by public systems supplying 130 or more litres per capita per day. Even in these towns, a significant proportion continues to be met from private sources. At the other end of the spectrum, only 60 per cent of Class III towns have such systems. There is considerable variation in the per capita supplies from public systems across and within towns.

Estimates of industrial consumption are based on limited data regarding requirements per unit of output in a few water-intensive industries. There is no comprehensive survey to determine the actual fresh-water consumption of industrial and commercial establishments, or of the sources from which this is met.

The above estimates of utilization relate to the gross volumes of water used by major sectors from man-made systems. Effective use for specific functional purposes is invariably less, and often much less, than gross usage. The balance—ranging from 10 per cent in some cases to as much as 80 per cent or more in some others—returns to the hydrological system as waste flow. A comprehensive and integrated picture of overall sources and use of water must take into account the fact that overall water availability in a region during a year is determined by natural rainfall. This not only determines supply from various man-made devices, but also meets a substantial part of the effective consumptive use of agricultural and non-agricultural uses, and the moisture needed to sustain the growth of forests and trees, and other vegetation, in uncultivated land. Account has also to be taken of losses due to natural evaporation that occurs from rain falling on the ground, from water flowing in rivers and streams, and water that accumulates in natural and man-made reservoirs. Adjustments have to be made for the volume of water that flows in from outside the country's boundaries net of what flows out of it.

The following table is an attempt to reconstruct an overall water balance for the country, taking into account all the above factors.

TABLE 10 Approximate Estimates of Sources and Uses of Water in India, *c.* 2000 (bcm)

Sources		Uses	
Precipitation[a]	4,000	Consumptive use by crops[b]	720
External[a]	600	Consumptive use: Forests and trees[c]	60
		Consumptive use: Non-agricultural[d]	30
		Non-consumptive evaporation and losses[e]	500
		Total utilization (sum of the above)	1,310
		Unutilized but utilizable[f]	470
		Evaporation from uncultivated fallow[g]	120
		Evaporation from water bodies[h]	70
		Non-functional evaporation/ untilizable[i]	1,500
		Outflow to other countries[j]	1,200
Total	4,600		4,600

Source: [a] CWC estimates.
Notes: [b] Guia 110 mha, with ET @ 0.294 m/ha and Gia of 75 mha ET @ 0.254 m/ha from rainfall and 0.295/ha from irrigation: m/ha. ET rates are author's estimates (Vaidyanathan and Sivasubramanaian 2004).

ᶜ Consumptive use of forests and permanent tree/plantations 73 mha ET @ 0.9 mha.

ᵈ Net use for non-agricultural purposes at 50 per cent of estimated gross use

ᵉ Difference between gross utilization and consumptive use of crops, forests/trees, and non-agricultural uses

ᶠ Difference between utilizable renewable freshwater (1,100 bcm) and utilized volume as of 2000 (830 bcm) as estimated by CWC

ᵍ Estimated evaporation from other vegetation on cultivable waste and fallow lands 39 mha @ 0.3 mha

ʰ Estimated evaporation from rivers and canals (196 thousand km: 20 metres width @ 0.5 mm/annum) and 7.4 mha of water bodies with ET @ 0.3 m; and evaporation from 212 back of live storage @ 0.2 m/annum

ⁱ CWC estimates of outflow.

ʲ Includes the difference between annual renewable supplies (1,870 bcm) and utilizable supplies (1,100 bcm) as estimated by the CWC. The balance is an unaccounted residual.

The total volume of renewable supplies of water from internal precipitation and inflows from outside the country is estimated at 4,600 bcm. Of this, roughly a quarter (1,200 bcm) flows out of the country and another 1,700 bcm is accounted by natural and non-functional evaporation or is unutilizable for various reasons. Supply available for use, 1,780 bcm, is thus barely two-fifths of total renewable supplies. Nearly three-fourths of it (or about 1,310 bcm) is currently utilized. Of this, effective utilization by crops, forests and trees, and for non-agricultural uses is estimated at some 800 bcm, the balance gives a rough measure of wastes and losses in the use of water for these purposes.

That this is a very rough and indicative exercise, subject to numerous caveats, needs hardly any emphasis. However, it does highlight some noteworthy features which help sum up the current state of play as regards the water balance in the country.

3

Impact of Water Resource Development on Agriculture

Irrigation impacts agriculture by (a) increasing the quantum, duration, and reliability of water available to crops beyond what is available from rainfall; (b) increasing the intensity of land use; (c) causing shifts in cropping patterns; and (d) raising the yield per hectare of individual crops.

Over this period, reported utilization of water from surface irrigation waterworks at the turn of the century is estimated to have increased nearly four times, and that of groundwater a little more than two-and-a-half times. As a result, irrigation has increased water supply per hectare of net irrigated land over and above the contribution of rainfall by around 800 to 1,000 m^3.

There are, of course, large regional variations in the magnitude of water utilization for agriculture as well as its growth overall, by source and per hectare of irrigated land. Available data do not permit exploration of these variations and their underlying reasons. However, some insights into their impact on the efficiency of water use can be obtained from an analysis of data on yields and consumptive use of water for irrigated and rainfed crops across regions, and over time.

Growth of Irrigated Area

In the early 1950s, out of the 125 mha of cultivated land, about one-sixth (22 mha) is reported to have been irrigated. It has since recorded a sustained increase, at the rate of 0.7 to 0.8 mha per annum. In 2006–7 out of a cultivated area of 141 mha (an increase of barely 10 per cent), about 62 mha (or about 45 per cent of total area) are irrigated.

The area reported to be served by tanks and other minor surface works has declined progressively over the period from 6.6 mha to 5.4 mha. However, the latest estimates put the figure at 7 mha, implying a substantial increase during the last decade. About a third of

TABLE 11 Trends in Net Irrigated Area by Source, 1950–2006 (mha)

	1950–1	1960–1	1970–1	1980–1	1990–1	2000–1	2006–7
Minor surface works	6.6	7	6.9	5.8	5.5	5.4	7.1
Canals	8.3	10.9	13	18.3	17.8	17	18
Tube wells	0	0.1	4.5	9.8	15.2	22.9	24
Other wells	7	7.2	7.4	8.2	10.9	11.3	12
Total	21	24	31	39	48	55	60

Source: Estimates published by Directorate of Economics and Statistics of the Ministry of Agriculture (various years).

the overall increase has come from large surface works, and a little over 10 per cent from open wells; much the larger part (70 per cent) has come from the expansion of tube well irrigation. The area irrigated by large canal systems has doubled during this period: from 8.3 mha to 18 mha. Most of this increase occurred between 1950 and 1980, and the pace has since slowed down. Open wells, which irrigated some 7 mha in 1950, now serve a little over 11 mha. There were no tube wells in the 1950s, and irrigated barely 100,000 ha in 1960. They now provide water to 24 mha, or about two-fifths of total irrigated land.

These data, though subject to caveats, highlight significant shifts in the source-wise distribution of irrigated area:

• Nearly three-fourths of the expansion in net irrigated area has come from groundwater. This is consistent with the progressive shift to borewells and deep tube wells, capable of tapping water from greater depths. Much of this expansion came in the 1970s and 1980s; thereafter the pace has slowed down considerably. This is largely because progressive overexploitation of groundwater has led to the rapid and widespread lowering of water tables, and a reduction in the area irrigated per well.

- About one-fourth of the increase in net irrigated area has come from the expansion of canal irrigated area. Again, much of this has come from the completion of a large number of projects during the 1970s and 1980s. However, the number of new projects completed thereafter, as well as the additions to potential, has come down sharply.

The progressive decline in the area under minor surface sources up to 2000 is consistent with the general impression that their condition is deteriorating due to neglect and many are derelict. However, more recent estimates of area irrigated by minor surface works show a reversal of these trends during the last decade or so. They also reflect substantial private investment in construction of new works in this category.

There are, of course, significant regional variations, both in the degree of development of different sources and their changes during the last three decades.

- Broadly speaking, states in the Indo-Gangetic Plain have the highest overall irrigation ratios, followed by

Andhra Pradesh and Tamil Nadu. Irrigation development is much lower than average in other parts of the country.

- In both periods, states that are better developed in terms of overall irrigation also tend to have higher proportions of cultivated land under both surface and groundwater.

- The proportion of net sown area irrigated by all sources and by groundwater has increased in all states. These increases are more marked in the Indo-Gangetic Plain than in other areas.

- The proportion of land served by surface sources has recorded a fall in many states; increases have been reported in central and western India, and the Deccan.

- In the early 1970s, interstate variations in overall irrigation ratio were more closely associated with variations in surface irrigation ratio rather than with groundwater ratio.

- Broadly speaking, regions which have recorded a reduction, or relatively smaller increases, in surface irrigation ratio tend to have bigger increases in groundwater.

Intensity of Cropping

Cropping intensity is measured by the ratio of gross cropped area to net cultivated area. On unirrigated land, crops can be grown only during the monsoon season. The kinds of crops that can be grown are also conditioned by the level of rainfall. Regions with low rainfall grow crops that require relatively less water, and crop mixtures that protect farmers against the precarious uncertainty of rain. Rainfed cropping in regions with relatively high rainfall (as in east India or the western coast) is also limited to the rainy season, but they grow water-intensive crops like paddy. Overall, the ratio of gross to net cultivated area under these conditions therefore tends to be low.

By increasing the quantum, assurance, and duration of water supply, irrigation makes it possible to grow crops that require more water and which take a longer time to mature. Because of this, the cropping intensity tends to increase as the proportion of irrigated to cultivated land increases. There is, in fact, a consistently strong positive correlation across regions between the irrigation ratio and the overall crop intensity. At the national level in the early 1950s, when the irrigation ratio was about 17 per cent, the ratio of gross to net crop area was about 1.1. The ratio has steadily increased since with the expansion of irrigation: in 2007 the irrigation ratio has reached 40 per cent, and the overall cropping intensity is around 1.45.

Its extent depends not just on the overall irrigation ratio but on the source, the extent to which it increases water supply, and also on agro-climatic conditions. In low rainfall regimes (such as is common in the western and north-western parts of the country), small-scale local surface storage (or lift irrigation) can supplement rainfall to a limited extent, and help farmers cope with dry spells, uncertain timings, and quantum of rain. In areas of more abundant rainfall, small-scale local works serve the same purpose; but they also permit more water-intensive crops (usually paddy) than is possible without irrigation. This is typically the case in much of south India in areas that get rain in both monsoons. But they can extend the cropping season only to a limited extent.

The picture changes significantly with access to irrigation from large surface storages and groundwater. Besides taking care of the uncertainties of rainfall in the main cropping season, large storages augment water supplies much more than small local works. They can carry over part of the storage to grow a winter crop, or even a limited summer crop, and raise longer-duration seasonal as well as annual crops (like sugar cane or bananas). Groundwater irrigation has similar effects; but its magnitude and pattern depend on the magnitude of water they can supply. Tube wells, especially deep tube wells, have much greater impact on cropping intensity than dug wells. This is more so in regions where surface and groundwater are used conjunctively.

The impact of irrigation on cropping intensity is the greatest in the low rainfall northwest regions, where most of the land is irrigated by surface water, along with groundwater recharged by it. A distinguishing feature of this region is that, besides increasing area under wheat and other rabi crops, it has led to extensive cultivation of water-intensive paddy in the kharif season.

Cropping Patterns

Irrigation brings about major changes in cropping patterns. Taking the country as a whole, the major part (over nearly 60 per cent) of the rainfed area is used to grow cereals other than rice and wheat, pulses, oilseeds, and cotton. Their share in irrigated crop area is barely one-fifth. Paddy accounts for close to 30 per cent of irrigated crop area, compared to 20 per cent in rainfed areas; wheat accounts for about 30 per cent (compared to a mere 3 per cent in rainfed areas). The share of long-duration crops like sugar cane, and high-value crops like sugar cane, condiments and spices, fruits and vegetables, and cotton, is much higher (around 15 per cent) compared to their share in unirrigated crop area (a mere 5 per cent). A substantial part of irrigated areas (about 12 per cent) grows oilseeds and fibres, but much less than their share in unirrigated areas (about 20 per cent). The extent and pattern of these shifts varies depending on the source of irrigation and also across regions.

In areas served by surface sources, the proportion of area growing kharif crops is much higher, and those under rabi and perennials much lower, compared to areas irrigated by groundwater. There are striking differences in the pattern among areas depending on different sources of groundwater. The proportion of area under rabi crops is much lower in dug well irrigated

areas than those watered by tube wells even as the proportion under kharif and perennial crops is much lower.
Deep tube wells have a larger extent of both rabi crops
and perennial crops compared to shallow tube wells.

TABLE 12 Cropping Patterns under Different Irrigation
Sources, All-India, 1993–4 (per cent)

	Kharif	Rabi	Perennials	Others	Total
Surface water	56.9	38.6	2.3	2.3	100
Groundwater total	34.8	56.4	5.3	3.5	100
Dug wells	21.3	73.7	3.4	1.6	100
Shallow tube wells	40.4	49.2	6.2	4.2	100
Deep tube wells	34	54.3	7.1	4.6	100

Source: GoI, Ministry of Agriculture, *Agriculture Census.*

Regional variations are also very pronounced. In Tamil
Nadu and Andhra Pradesh, most (85 per cent) of the
rainfed crop area is devoted to other cereals, pulses,
oilseeds, and cotton. Paddy, which is a relatively minor
crop under rainfed conditions, is the dominant crop,
covering more than half the total crop area under
irrigation. The share of oilseeds and cotton under irrigation is comparable to rainfed land. With irrigation,
there is a big shift towards long-duration and high-
value crops (especially sugar cane and fruits). The share
of other cereals, pulses, oilseeds, and fibres is much less
than under rainfed conditions. In both states, rainfed

cropping patterns are more diversified—both in terms of the variety of crops and the distribution of area—than under irrigation.

In Odisha, Bengal, and Bihar, rice is the dominant crop on both irrigated and rainfed lands. In Odisha and Bengal, the proportion of irrigated area under this crop is significantly higher than on unirrigated land. There is also a pronounced shift to the cultivation of fruits and vegetables. In Bengal, the area under wheat shows a marginal rise. However, the shift towards other long-duration and high-value crops is not striking. Here again, rainfed cropping patterns are more diversified than with irrigation.

In Bihar, the proportion of paddy in irrigated areas is less than under rainfed conditions. The most striking change is a huge shift towards wheat production, and a moderate shift towards fruits and vegetables. A similar pattern is evident in Uttar Pradesh and Madhya Pradesh; but the proportion of area devoted to paddy as well as the difference between irrigated and rainfed areas is much lower, even as the shift to wheat is much larger than in Bihar. The shift towards sugar cane and, to a lesser extent, fruits and vegetables, on irrigated lands is more striking in Uttar Pradesh than in Bihar.

In all these states, the share of other cereals in irrigated area is much higher than under unirrigated land; but in Bihar, a substantially large proportion is used to grow pulses on both categories of land. Irrigated cropping patterns are less diversified compared to rainfed land in all cases.

The shift towards wheat from traditional dryland crops under irrigation is also evident in Punjab and Haryana. But the more striking feature is paddy, which cannot be grown with their rainfall, and yet takes up about a fifth of the irrigated area in Haryana, and nearly a third in Punjab. Both have become the rice bowls of India. In Punjab, irrigation leads to less-diversified cropping patterns.

Changes in cropping patterns under irrigation show a very different pattern in Gujarat, Maharashtra, and Rajasthan. With irrigation, the proportion of area under both rice and wheat increases in all three, but the shift in rice is much smaller than towards wheat, especially in Madhya Pradesh. The proportion of area under sugar cane and high-value crops increases in all three, but in varying degrees. In all three of them, irrigation leads to much greater diversification of crops than in most states.

Overall both irrigated and rainfed cropping patterns seem to have become more diversified, but in varying degrees. There have also been shifts in both irrigated and rainfed cropping patterns over time, reflecting changes in the demand, relative prices, and relative yields.

Crop Yields

Irrigation provides more water to crops than is available from rainfall. Allowing for various losses and waste, it is estimated to contribute somewhat over a half of the estimated total consumptive use of water of irrigated crops in the country. Besides increasing cropping intensity and diversifying cropping patterns towards water-intensive crops that yield more, and command a higher market value, irrigation plays a crucial role in increasing the yields of individual crops by enabling them to absorb more nutrients and convert them into usable biomass with greater efficiency than is possible under rainfed conditions. The cumulative impact of these factors results in overall value of production per hectare of irrigated land being much higher than that of rainfed crops.

Estimates of overall yields of specific crops are made and published regularly, both at the state and district levels. Estimates of overall per hectare yields of irrigated and rainfed areas are available only for a few major crops, and that too only at the state level. The bases of state- and district-level estimates are very different. The methods used, the care with which data are collected, and their accuracy cannot be considered satisfactory. Nevertheless, they do provide some idea of the overall production per hectare of irrigated and unirrigated land at the state level for a few periods.

On a rough estimate (Vaidyanathan 2010), taking the country as a whole, irrigated crops accounted for roughly 60 per cent of total value of crop output in the early 1990s. Across states, the contribution of irrigated crops to total output ranges between 35 per cent or less (Odisha and Madhya Pradesh) and over 90 per cent (Haryana and Punjab). Nearly three-fourths of the increase in the country's total output between the early 1970s and early 1990s has come from irrigated crops. In most states, the major part of increase in output is on account of irrigated crops, the proportion ranging from around 40–50 per cent in some (Karnataka and

Odisha) to over 90 per cent in a few (including Punjab and Haryana). These variations reflect differences in both the extent of increase in irrigated area relative to total crop area and also in the relative rates of increase in per hectare yields.

The impact of irrigation on crop yields varies a great deal between crops and across regions. Rough estimates suggest that, for the country as a whole, overall output per hectare of irrigated crop area (in the early 1990s) was about two-and-half times that of unirrigated crops. While production value per hectare of irrigated crops overall and for paddy, wheat, and cotton are in most cases higher than that of rainfed crops, the difference ranges from about as low as 20 per cent in some to more than 300 per cent in a few. These variations high-light the cumulative effect of differences in climate, the sources of irrigation, and the nature and extent of shifts in cropping patterns as a result of irrigation.

The importance of rainfall as a factor determining the level of, and the differential between, land productivity in unirrigated and rainfed areas is brought out by comparing average yield in districts grouped by rainfall and level of rainfall. Among districts with lower than average levels of irrigation, yields are lowest in those with low rainfall and highest in the group with high rainfall. In all rainfall groups, districts with higher levels of irrigation use more fertilizers, and report much higher yields. The difference in yields between low and high irrigation is the highest, both in absolute and relative terms. In the low rainfall areas, the average yields in high-irrigation tracts are about twice those in the low-irrigation group; in medium rainfall zones, high-irrigation groups get 80–90 per cent higher yields compared to low irrigation districts; in high rainfall districts, yield in tracts with better-developed irrigation is only 30 per cent higher than in areas with low irrigation ratios. Over time, the differential that irrigation makes has widened in all rainfall zones.

Productivity differentials and share of irrigated crops in total output are seen to be high in states (Rajasthan, Gujarat) which have relatively low rainfall, moderate levels of irrigation, and high levels of groundwater use; and in Haryana, and Punjab (low rainfall, very high level of irrigation and of conjunctive use of surface and groundwater), and UP (a high level of groundwater-dominant irrigation).

Being the ultimate source of supply for surface storages and, to a lesser extent, from groundwater,

TABLE 13 Overall Crop Yields and Levels of Irrigation and Fertilizers in Different Regions Classified according to Level of Rainfall and Irrigation, 1962–5 to 1991–3

	GVO/GCA				GIA/GCA per cent			Fertilizers (kg of nutrients/ha)		
	1960s	1970s	1980s	1990s	1970s	1980s	1990s	1970s	1980s	1990s
LL	2,427	2,567	3,473	4,282	11	20	21	9	20	45
LH	4,345	5,398	6,912	9,443	46	52	57	25	60	93
MI	2,931	3,070	3,915	5,025	12	18	24	10	24	56
MH	4,845	5,568	7,020	9,648	40	49	58	25	61	104
HL	3,578	3,842	4,207	5,981	9	14	23	8	20	52
HH	4,655	5,156	5,969	8,146	38	46	47	23	45	104

Source: Author's estimate (see Vaidyanathan 2004).

Notes: GVO refers to gross value of output; GCA refers to gross crop area; GIA refers to gross irrigated area.

the vagaries of rainfall also affect the volume of water availability for irrigation. In surface irrigated areas, the volume of inflows available for irrigation and its distribution depends on the level of rainfall in their catchments, its seasonal distribution, and their variability. These factors also have a significant bearing on the extent of increase in crop yields during the main crop season, the extension of cropping into the drier seasons as well as the nature and extent of cropping pattern shifts that irrigation makes possible. In all these respects, large reservoirs and diversion canal systems that tap rainfall from wide catchments and areas using groundwater are better placed than small storages and diversion works.

Efficiency of Water Use

Efficiency of water use has two components: (a) the proportion of gross volume of water used by crops that goes to meet their consumptive use; and (b) the difference it makes to crop yields per hectare and per unit of consumptive use. The former is an index of technical efficiency and the latter of productive efficiency.

Technical Efficiency

'Consumptive use' of a crop is the amount of water which transpires through its leaves in the course of its growth and which evaporates from wetted surfaces in fields where it is grown. The quantum of this transpiration is called 'evapotranspiration' (ET). It is well established that there is an upper limit to ET which, for most crops, is equal to potential evaporation (PE) that occurs naturally from a free open surface of water. Its magnitude depends on sunshine, rainfall, temperatures, humidity, and other climatic features which are highly variable across seasons and regions. Direct measurements of PE using calibrated devices—like pan evapometers and lysimeters—are available for selected centres. But more detailed daily and seasonal estimates under varying agro-climatic conditions based on theoretically validated relationships between climatic variables and PE are available.

Given this, the quantum of PE that occurs during the period of growth of different crops in different regions can also be estimated. ET of crops is in most cases, with the exception of paddy, equal to or less than PE. ET and the ratio of ET to PE for crops varies across different climate regimes, seasons, and the duration of their growth. These can be estimated using crop and climatic region-specific coefficients worked out by the Food and Agriculture Organization (FAO). The coefficients for most seasonal crops are less than 1; and equal to 1 for crops like sugar cane. For paddy, which needs a lot of standing water in the field, the coefficient value is 1.2. Based on these coefficients, crop group-wise and season-wise estimates of consumptive use have been made for a few recent points of time for different agro-climatic regions. It needs to be emphasized that these empirical estimates are necessarily approximate.

Consumptive use of unirrigated crops has to be met wholly from the contribution of local rainfall to building soil moisture. Rainfed areas cannot grow crops whose consumptive use requirements exceed the soil moisture built by rainfall. Crops that can be grown have also to contend with both shortages of soil moisture during their growth due to uneven intra-seasonal distribution of rain and also risks of crop failure due to failure of rainfall. These factors affect the large variations in rainfed cropping patterns across rainfall zones.

Irrigated crops use moisture from rainfall as well as irrigation. The contribution of irrigation to their consumptive use is the difference between their total ET and available moisture from rainfall. Rough estimates based on official statistics of district-wise crop areas, their seasonal distribution and ET rates, and total consumptive use in the early 1990s averaged around 2,750 m^3 per hectare of rainfed crops and 5,490 m^3 per hectare of irrigated crops, of which around 56 per cent was met from rainfall and the balance from irrigation. Of the total gross utilization of water from irrigated crops from surface and groundwater (reported at around 523 bcm), about 200 bcm goes to meet their consumptive use. On this basis, the technical efficiency of use of irrigation supplies is around 36 per cent overall and varies between 26 and 27 per cent in major peninsular river basins to nearly 55 per cent in Tapti, Narmada, and other west-flowing rivers (Vaidyanathan 2006). That these are rough and indicative measures which leave much room for refinement needs hardly any emphasis.

The difference between gross utilization and consumptive use of irrigation water gives a measure of losses in conveyance and distribution due to evaporation and seepage, leakages from damaged or broken

banks of canals and distributaries into man-made or
natural wetlands and swamps in the command, and
from wasteful evaporation. Efficiency of utilization
is likely to vary between different kinds of projects,
depending on the characteristics of soil and climate
in the command, on how extensive the distribution
network is, how well it is maintained and on the care
with which water is managed in the field. The larger
the command area, the larger are the likely losses and
the lower the efficiency. Efficiency is likely to be
higher in canal commands where the conjunctive use
of groundwater is widespread. It will be much higher
in the case of wells and tube wells because their command area is relatively small, and water has to traverse
much shorter distances from the wellhead to the field.
Since they provide greater control over the timing and
quantum of application of water, on-field losses are
also reduced. This is more so when water is distributed
through pipes and through drip systems.

There is a widespread belief that lining of canals
and distributaries and or laying concrete pipelines will
improve efficiency by reducing groundwater recharge
seepage losses. But apart from its cost-effectiveness,
reduced seepage reduction would result in reduced

groundwater recharge in command areas and the possibilities of recycling seepage for conjunctive use groundwater. Better maintenance of distribution networks and devices to regulate the flow of water to different sections would undoubtedly improve efficient use of available supplies by reducing leakages and increasing supplies to crops. There is some evidence that part of the reason for the low technical efficiency in use of irrigation is that a large proportion of water from surface systems is supplied during the kharif season when the deficit between ET and supply from rainfall is relatively small and, in fact, rainfall exceeds ET in many areas. This aspect needs more careful study.

Yields per Unit of Water Use

Output per hectare is everywhere higher under irrigation than under rainfed conditions. This is partly because the proportion of area devoted to water-intensive, high-value, and long-duration crops is much higher under irrigation than in rainfed tracts. While irrigated yields for specific crops are also higher than under unirrigated conditions, the realized irrigated yields are known to be much below potential. A more meaningful measure of the efficiency of irrigation is the quantum of crop output value per unit of consumptive use.

Given agro-climatic conditions, consumptive use per hectare of particular crops in a season is more or less constant. The level of biochemical inputs is variable. Given the synergetic effects of irrigation in combination with biotechnology and associated inputs, one would expect that under optimal soil moisture regimes and proper management of inputs, output per unit of consumptive use of water on irrigated areas would be substantially higher than under rainfed conditions. Available evidence gives a mixed picture.

The expectation that the output per unit of consumptive use will be higher under irrigation is strongly corroborated for cotton in all states where it is a significant crop (the difference ranging between 20 per cent and 175 per cent). This also the case for paddy in a majority of states—the difference ranges between 35 per cent and 100 per cent. In a couple of states, estimated output per unit of consumptive use of rainfed paddy is higher, but these regions where the crop is grown have high rainfall, and the demarcation of irrigated and rainfed crops is rather problematic. In the case of wheat, this index for irrigated areas is invariably less than for the unirrigated crops. This could be because the rabi season has little rainfall, and unirrigated wheat is cultivated using residual soil moisture carried over from the kharif season (Vaidyanathan 2006).

A major reason for this is that improved varieties, fertilizers, and other biophysical inputs work in synergy with the quality of water management. The synergy is the greatest—and realized yields closest to potential—when water (from rainfall and irrigation) is managed to ensure that adequate moisture is available in the soil to meet the ET of crops at all times, especially during the critical phases of their growth. This calls for regulation in the timing and quantum of irrigation during the critical phases of growth. This is difficult to achieve in surface irrigation systems that serve large command areas, growing many different crops by a large number of farmers. This calls for a degree of sophistication in design of distribution systems and in their management for which most systems are simply not equipped. Such regulation is easier for wells and tube wells which have smaller commands and whose owners can control the timing and quantum of pumping according the conditions of crops. Given the limitations of estimates of irrigated and rainfed yields, and the possibility of other factors influencing their relative magnitudes, these conclusions are at best indicative. There is clearly a need for closer analysis, using better data.

Despite these problems, there is little doubt that much of the transformation of Indian agriculture from relative stagnation to one of sustained, if modest, growth of agricultural production has been made possible by the spread of irrigation. For many decades before Independence, agriculture was mostly dependent on rainfall. Only a small portion was irrigated by sources (local tanks, streams, and dug wells) that provided limited and uncertain supplements to rain. In the absence of any significant improvement in agricultural technology, overall yields were low, and did not see sustained increase. Production was largely a function of cultivated area. There was considerable cultivable but uncultivated land which could be brought under the plough to accommodate increases in population. However, population growth during those times was itself rather slow compared to later periods. Overall, production growth barely kept pace with that of population, and was prone to fluctuation depending on the proverbial vagaries of rainfall.

The post-Independence period saw a decisive break from these trends. During the last six decades, crop production has shown sustained growth, at an average rate of around 2.6–2.7 per cent per year. In the early phases of this period, expansion of cultivated area was the main source of growth; yield improvement accounted for a smaller part of it. Over time, the scope for expanding cultivated land has declined progressively, and more or less reached the limit. Its contribution to growth has also declined progressively, and that of yield improvement increased. Much of the increase in the latter phases of this period has come from more intensive use of land (reflected in the growth of double-cropped area), shifts in cropping pattern towards higher-yielding and more valuable crops, and an increase in per hectare yields of many important crops. These changes have been made possible by massive investments in irrigation (which have led to a huge increase in the proportion of irrigated to total crop area), improvements in its quality because of the rapid growth of groundwater use, together with major improvements in biochemical technology for crop husbandry.

4

Problems of Implementation and Management

Post-Independence expansion in the availability of water for irrigation and non-agricultural uses is both impressive and unprecedented. Its contribution to increased agricultural production is unquestionably very important. However, experience has also uncovered many issues about the strategy being followed, its implementation, and impact. Persistent large gaps between targets and achievements, huge escalation in costs, increasing delays in the completion of projects, the fact that the impact on agricultural productivity has been less than expected, are all matters of concern. Inadequate attention has been given to providing safe and assured water supply for domestic and non-agricultural uses. Increasing conflicts over access to and the use of water, and the inability to manage them; apprehensions of looming water scarcity; the failure to address the adverse environmental impact of water resource projects; the fiscal and economic consequences of policies for pricing of water, and the efficient and sustainable use of water, are all matters of serious concern.

Problems in Implementation

Under the Indian Constitution, the development and management of water resources is the responsibility of state governments. Projects on interstate rivers are, however, required to be approved by the central government. The Centre is also authorized by law to devise mechanisms for the settlement of disputes between riparian states over the sharing of water in interstate rivers, and requires states to provide data on water resources and their utilization in their domain, as well as set up organizations for integrated planning of water use of river basins.

In the early phases of planning, the Centre had a great deal of influence in shaping the country's water resource planning strategy generally, and large-scale surface works in particular. It established a strong professional organization for identifying potential sites, conducting preparatory surveys, and preparing detailed designs for large projects. It played an important role in providing technical support and advice to states in the design and construction of many schemes. The Centre also set up several tribunals to decide on the allocation of the waters of major interstate rivers between riparian states. Their awards were accepted as binding, and have been observed till recently.

The Planning Commission also had a significant role in shaping the overall water resource development strategy and priorities, and in determining the scale and content of state programmes. The size, content, and financial outlays of state plans, including water resource projects, as well as the quantum of central assistance to be provided to each state annually and for each plan period were decided by the Commission after extensive discussions with state ministers and officials. All major water resource projects had to be approved by the commission on the basis of a techno-economic appraisal by a technical advisory committee before they could be implemented. Revisions in scope, design, and cost estimates of major projects were also subject to central review and approval. The states were, however, free to decide on schemes for minor irrigation works and for the development of groundwater.

Over time, the Centre's leverage in regulating and monitoring state water resource programmes generally and major and medium projects in particular, has progressively weakened for many reasons: the information provided at the time of formulating annual and five-year plans focused more on financial outlays than on the progress of the physical works. Critical assessments of the justification for large revisions in design and costs, and concrete measures for speedier implementation have come to receive less and less attention. States have been increasingly reluctant to provide data needed by the Planning Commission and the Central Water Commission (CWC) to monitor the progress of projects.

Central assistance for irrigation is given to the states without any effective mechanism to define and enforce transparent contracting procedures. Review mechanisms for assessing the causes of delays, the justification for larger outlays, and the monitoring of the actual progress of works on the ground have become more and more lax. This has been compounded by resistance to supervision by the Centre of the use of allocated plan funds, and the assertion of the states' right to take up irrigation projects without the Planning Commission's approval. The Centre is powerless to check expenditure on unauthorized projects.

Central government agencies are neither willing, nor equipped, to exercise the authority that they have under law to verify what is happening on the ground, or to ensure the strict observance of protocols for the appraisal of project proposals. The practice of preparing completion reports on all major projects (mandatory in the pre-Independence period), which is important for learning from experience and avoiding mistakes in the future, was given up. Achievements in terms of area irrigated by different sources as reported by state statistical agencies (including the data generated by the periodic minor irrigation censuses) are accepted without any attempt at independent verification. Significant divergence between estimates of expected and actual achievements revealed by different agencies has not evoked any serious effort to explore the reasons or put in place mechanisms for independent and objective assessments.

These tendencies have been reinforced by the growing politicization of decisions regarding investments in publicly funded irrigation projects. Over the years, faced with the surge of ground-level demand for irrigation, political expediency has led state governments to commit themselves to taking up a large number of new projects. The states did not pay sufficient attention to building capacity for preparatory investigations of standards necessary for the careful designing of the engineering projects and their operations. On the contrary, with mounting political pressures to take up more and more projects, the quality of investigation and design deteriorated. These pressures also led to a dilution of the rigour with which their technical features and economic viability were scrutinized by the technical advisory committee and the Planning Commission before approval.

As a result, revisions in scope, design, and cost estimates became more and more frequent, and larger in magnitude. The completion of projects got delayed. This process intensified during the 1970s and 1980s, and has grown to unmanageable proportions during the last two decades. It is significant that, of the 500 major and medium projects spilling over into the Twelfth Plan, as many as 300 have been taken up and implemented without the Planning Commission's approval; as many as a third of the projects taken up during the last two decades are incomplete; and the latest estimate of their costs is nearly five times the original estimate.

Average annual plan outlay on major and medium projects at current prices has increased more than five-fold during the last three decades: from Rs 300 billion in the 1980s, to over Rs 1,500 billion during the Tenth and Eleventh plans. Much of this is accounted for by the rise in costs due to inflation, changes in scope and design of projects after they have been approved, and the growing number of incomplete projects, both approved and unapproved. The number of incomplete projects relative to completed ones has increased from 5 per cent in 1960, to 10 per cent in 1980 and 1990, and over a third subsequently. As a result, the pace of expansion in irrigation potential from these projects has come down sharply during the 1980s and 1990s despite the large increase in outlays, both in nominal and real terms. Additions to their irrigation potential, as estimated by states, are far from commensurate with the increase in outlay and have, in fact, slowed down since the 1980s.

There is no central monitoring of even public sector programmes for minor surface works. States do not have reliable, updated data on the number of such works and their conditions or about the area they irrigate. Sizeable amounts have been spent by the public sector, ostensibly for the rehabilitation and improvement of existing tanks and the construction of new works. Official land-use statistics show a progressive decline in the area irrigated by these works. However, as much as Rs 460 billion has been spent on these works over the last six decades. According to the Planning Commission, this has added 9 mha to irrigation potential. The bases of both these estimates are questionable. A large number of minor surface works constructed by the private sector does not even find a mention in the plans.

Groundwater irrigation, whose importance as a source of irrigation has increased rapidly, is almost entirely in the private sector. Estimates of the area irrigated by wells and tube wells based on village records are at variance with estimates of the minor irrigation censuses and estimates of potential as reported by the Planning Commission. Getting reliable estimates of this source is particularly difficult given their huge number, the significant and continuing changes in the composition of wells and lifting devices of different types, the trend towards the use of more and more powerful pumps, and falling water tables. Another problem is that they do not make any distinction between areas that use groundwater as the sole source of irrigation and those used in conjunction with surface water.

Underutilization of Irrigation Potential

A recurrent criticism of the performance of irrigation programmes is the persistent and growing underutilization of the potential created by completed projects. Planning Commission estimates also show persistent and increasing shortfall of utilization relative to potential (measured by gross irrigated area), both overall and for different sources: this gap for all sources has grown progressively from less than 5 per cent of potential in the 1960s to 15 per cent currently. Much of this shortfall is on account of major and medium projects: the degree of under-utilization of their potential has increased from around 8 per cent in the 1960s to 19 per cent in recent years.

In the case of both minor surface works and groundwater, estimated utilization is reported to be close to potential till the 1980s but thereafter underutilization,

though small, has been rising. The area potentially irri-
gable by major and medium surface irrigation projects
is worked out on the basis of estimated seasonal volume
of water inflows into the reservoir, and assumptions
about cropping patterns and their water requirements
as approved at the time of their clearance. Experience
shows that assumptions regarding all these aspects on
which projects are designed are generally not realized
when they go into operation.

Delays in completion of distribution channels
to carry water from tertiary outlets to the fields and
preparing lands for irrigated farming are widely cited
reasons for underutilization. Command area development programmes are meant to expedite the process
through public investment. But hard evidence about
their effectiveness is inadequate. A more important
reason is that actual inflows into the reservoir and
their seasonal patterns turn out to be different and
more volatile than expected. So do cropping patterns
because project designs generally do not take into
account the possibilities of conjunctive use of surface
and groundwater, and also because considerations of
relative profitability result in larger area under more
profitable but more water-intensive crops than envis-

aged. Moreover, the Planning Commission estimates of the area irrigated do not take into account the effect of increasing incidence of unauthorized tapping of canal waters for irrigating areas outside the command.

The basis for Planning Commission estimates of potential and realized gross irrigated area from minor surface works and groundwater are far more opaque. Till the 1980s, the two estimates are the same, but thereafter utilization is shown to be below potential, with the gap increasing progressively. Given the difficulties inherent in assessing the potential of the huge number and diverse types of these sources, and in the absence of any mechanism for systematic monitoring of their functioning, their credibility is questionable. Of late, the minor irrigation censuses provide estimates of both potential and actual irrigated areas of these sources. The procedures and practical problems of the potential and actual area irrigated by each individual work enumerated by the census are hugely daunting.

The Planning Commission's estimate of actual utilization in terms of gross area irrigated by all sources differs substantially from land-use statistics published by the Ministry of Agriculture and by the National

Sample Survey. Its estimates of both potential and utilization of minor surface works (10.4 mha and 7 mha, respectively, in 2001–2) are substantially lower than those of the MI census of 2001 (13.6 mha and 10.4 mha). This is also the case for groundwater whose potential, according to the Planning Commission, was 45 mha (compared to 58 mha in the MI census) and utilization 38 mha (as against the MI census figure of 45 mha).

The coverage, concepts, and procedures used by different sources for the compilation of data are not comparable. Moreover, there are serious questions about the reliability of estimates based on data compiled by village officials. They are overloaded with numerous functions; the importance attached to supervised collection of land-use and crop data has been greatly reduced; and mechanisms for verification of the records are ineffective. There are ambiguities in the categorization of irrigation sources with considerable scope for errors of omission, commission, and bias in reporting. Neither the Planning Commission nor the official land-use statistics cover all minor irrigation sources, nor do they take cognizance of the unauthorized and illegal diversion or pumping of water from canals and rivers. There is reason to believe that the latter is becoming more and more widespread.

Given deficiencies and non-comparability of the coverage and basis for estimates made by different agencies, meaningful comparison of these estimates is not possible. It is difficult to judge which of them is closest to reality.

Management Problems

Deficiencies in both the organization and management of water in India affect the efficiency with which it is utilized. Major and medium surface systems are managed entirely by government officials, mostly engineers. The delimitation of command areas, rules regarding water entitlements, permissible cropping patterns, scheduling of canal supplies, and the extraction of groundwater in the command is entirely the government's prerogative. These rules—sometimes in the form of a statute but, for the most part, through executive orders—are generally based on assumptions regarding water availability and cropping patterns at the time of construction. They are usually quite general, and do not explicitly indicate how they will be adjusted under various contingencies, especially in times of shortfalls in water supply to the system. The rationale underlying the rules, and the process of making and changing them, are seldom spelt out and made known to stakeholders. The entitlements of individual users are ill-defined and non-enforceable. There are no institutionalized mechanisms for consultation with stakeholders in making and changing rules, nor for dealing with and redressing their complaints in a transparent manner.

Canals and distribution networks tend to deteriorate due to poor maintenance, and natural and man-made damages. Maintenance of these systems is the exclusive responsibility of the states, to be met out of their regular budgets. Revenues from water charges are treated as part of the overall revenue pool of state governments whose disposition is decided by their finance departments. Allocations for recurrent expenditures of irrigation departments have been inadequate, both for maintenance and repair as well as for operational staff. Of late, as part of an effort to bring about a major restructuring of water management in public systems, some states have taken the initiative to involve user associations in maintenance. Incentives to do so have been undertaken by providing funds from the budget directly, or by empowering them to collect water charges, and retain a part of these for maintenance. These are relatively recent initiatives, and limited in scale. The results are reported to be encouraging. However, they need to be monitored independently to assess their performance and impact over a period of time.

Large canal systems have to deliver water to a large number of users, spread over extensive areas, and growing diverse crops. Moreover, not all of these are constant, responding as they do to changes in rainfall, water flows into the system, and the market environment. Under these conditions, it is physically and logistically very difficult to ensure that water deliveries meet the requirements of individual users in all parts of the command. The capacity for flexible adaptation to meet changing situations is also severely limited. For this reason, systems tend to work out the timing and duration of water deliveries to different segments of the command, based on the cropping patterns considered appropriate for the use of available water at the time of the design and approval of each project.

Operational rules also specify the kinds of crops, especially the area under water-intensive crops that can be grown in different sections of the command. Rules also provide for penalties for violations of crop-pattern restrictions and the unauthorized extraction of water from reservoirs and canals. The government and system managers have the authority to adapt and modify the rules of allocation and scheduling. But this is used mostly to adjust the dates of opening the reservoirs and the frequency and duration of supplies, depending on actual rainfall and water inflows into the reservoirs in a season and year. Major changes in allocation rules—taking into account ground reality and to accommodate new claims—are rare, and are decided by the government on political considerations, quite unmindful of the impact on overall productivity.

In practice, systems seldom conform to the for-mal rules. Violations of cropping pattern regulations, unauthorized diversions from distribution channels, and outright theft of canal water to charge wells are widespread. Extraction of groundwater from wells and tube wells within canal command areas is wide-spread, despite restrictions. Over the years, pumping from rivers directly or from wells and borewells dug in riverbeds, has become increasingly widespread. That the phenomenon is widespread and increasing is well known to the government and the water bureaucracy. Some of it is done with the explicit authorization of the government; much else without it. System managers are pressured not to enforce rules against violators, or to levy and recover penalties. Strict enforcement is not considered politically expedient by local politicians or the higher echelons of government. This leaves ample room for pressuring officials to manipulate the quantum and timing of water deliveries, and/or to condone violations of rules by influential individuals and vocal groups.

In an attempt to improve the quality of water management, the National Water Management Programme was launched in the 1980s. It installed telecom networks to facilitate communication between field level and higher-tier functionaries. There were also plans to use remote-sensing satellites to regulate water distribution between different segments of the command, based on real-time information on segments facing water stress. The results have not been evaluated. In any case, the project has been discontinued. The deeper problems—the rigidity and deficiencies of outdated operating rules, and the restructuring of institutional arrangements for water management—were not addressed.

The focus has since shifted to user participation in the management of surface systems. Several states have made it mandatory to set up water user associations (WUAs) at the tertiary level. The expectation was that they would facilitate active involvement in maintenance and repair, better collection of water rates, and in more efficient use of water. It was expected that this would provide for interaction between users and system management. Some states have given the WUAs the responsibility for maintenance and repair, along with some budgetary funds, and the collection of water charges. The results are reported to be impressive in Andhra Pradesh. In Tamil Nadu—which pioneered this approach—they have played a significant role in getting the system managers to address users' problems, both at the local and system levels. However, since they have no control over when and how much water will be available at the tertiary level, WUAs cannot be expected to make any significant impact on improving water-use efficiency. That calls for a much more drastic restructuring of management at the system level.

A few states, notably Andhra Pradesh, Maharashtra, and Odisha, have made attempts in this direction.

They have enacted legislation which provides for elected user representatives to participate in management committees at all levels, right up to the apex of the systems. The power to make and change allocation rules, and decide on water rates continues to vest with the government, subject to review by an independent regulatory agency. The effective implementation of the spirit of the legislation has, however, been tardy, in the face of resistance both from the political class and the irrigation bureaucracy. The reluctance to address the problem of raising water rates to more economical levels remains a serious impediment to reform.

Minor surface irrigation works are of two kinds: community-managed works, and those left to the private sector. The latter are far more important than is believed. They include works serving many users as well as a large and increasing number of relatively small lift irrigation works. Very little is known about or how they are managed or about the role of the state in regulating them.

Community-managed works are relatively old. Maintenance and regulation of water distribution of most of them are managed by user communities with varying degrees of effectiveness and ability to adapt to societal and technological changes. Arrangements for managing water allocation and shortages within a season seem to work reasonably well, though they are not free from conflict. This is facilitated by the fact that ayacuts are small, and that operations are closely monitored by users. But, given the conditions of water supply and the quality of the distribution networks, the ability to regulate water deliveries to maintain an optimal soil moisture regime is even more limited than with large systems.

Plans provide for rehabilitation and modernization programmes for tanks involving substantial outlays, funded domestically and by foreign donors. Numerous studies have pointed to serious deficiencies in these programmes, most of which reflect a lack of accountable and transparent implementation. The works are planned by government engineers and implemented through contractors, without any involvement, or even consultation with, the communities they serve.

Most wells and tube wells are privately owned and operated. They are a significant source of water supply for domestic and non-agricultural uses. But little is known about their number or the volume of water extracted by them. The phenomenal expansion of irrigation wells has been facilitated by a proactive government policy of encouraging the process. While the number wells and the volume of water extracted has increased, the natural rate of recharge is more or less constant. As volumes extracted have increased, water tables have begun dropping. Individual farmers have responded by deepening their wells/tube wells, and using more powerful pumps to prevent reduction in the volume available to them. Sustained reduction in the depth of the water table reflected in the increasing depth of wells, more powerful pumps, and reduced yields per well, are indicative of extraction exceeding normal rates of recharge.

The responsibility for tracking these trends and taking corrective measures, however, vests exclusively with the states. But they have done little to contain the surging demand for groundwater for irrigation. In the face of the intense and unrelenting pressure from farmers, they have not exercised such regulatory authority as they have under law; also, given the huge number of widely dispersed wells, enforcement is impossible. On the other hand, the policy of supplying electricity at nominal or near-free rates has had exactly the opposite effect: by increasing private returns on investment, it has encouraged the rapid expansion of groundwater exploitation beyond sustainable levels.

There are indications that shortages of power, and its uncertain supply, have led to a significant increase in the proportion of wells and tube wells using diesel. Though diesel itself is heavily subsided, its price is higher than that of electricity. The costs of pumping must, therefore, have increased. There has been a progressive slowing down in the rate of expansion of potential, especially in the last decade. The degree of underutilization was less than 5 per cent in the mid-1980s, but currently it is about 10 per cent.

The MI census reports about one in eight dug wells is currently out of use. 'Less water discharge' is cited as the most important reason. The area actually irrigating them is only 40 per cent of their estimated potential. Most tube wells (both shallow and deep) are functional, but some report inadequate water. However, both report substantial under-utilization of potential: about 20 per cent in shallow and nearly a third in deep tube wells. All this suggests a decline in the quantum of water extracted per well/tube well. This is corroborated by the fact that the increase in groundwater use for irrigation, as estimated by the Central Ground Water

Board (CGWB), is much slower than the reported growth of irrigated areas. A more definitive assessment of the magnitude of decline in different categories of wells and regions calls for validated data based on the proper measurement of extraction rates that are not available so far.

5

Water Pricing Policies

Governments have a pervasive role not only in the development and management of water resources and electricity, and the regulation of their allocation between uses and users, but also in determining the price at which they are supplied to users. During the post-Independence period, governments have followed a deliberate policy of supplying water from public systems and the energy used for irrigation at rates well below cost, and have been progressively lowering them even as costs have been rising. This has had far-reaching deleterious consequences for the efficient and sustainable use of water, and has seen a huge and growing burden on the fisc.

In the early phases of colonial rule, governments were not willing to invest public funds in irrigation unless it could provide a reasonable rate of financial return after covering operating costs. Except for 'protective' works in areas liable to severe droughts and recurrent famines, this condition was more or less strictly observed in approving public investments in 'productive' works. The idea that besides its direct contribution to increased agricultural production, irrigation has significant indirect beneficial impacts on the rural economy gained gradual recognition. Under planning, social cost-benefit analysis came to be officially accepted as the basis for public investment decisions. Initially, the idea was that the beneficiaries of public irrigation projects should meet the costs incurred on providing water. Besides water charges based on the area irrigated under different crops according to season and water intensity, most states also passed legislation requiring beneficiaries to pay a betterment levy to capture a part of the increase in productivity and the capital value of land due to irrigation. In the early 1970s, the National Irrigation Commission appointed by the Government of India underscored the importance of securing an adequate return from investment in irrigation projects, and recommended that water rates be fixed at levels that would cover working expenses and interest charges.

However, state governments did not comply with these guidelines. The requirement regarding a minimum rate of financial return was dropped on the grounds that the indirect and social benefits from irrigation were substantial, and that farmers, being poor, could not afford to pay full costs, and therefore deserved to be subsidized. Much the same argument was used to justify much lower electricity rates for agricultural use than the cost of supplying power to rural areas, and using higher rates for non-agricultural uses to compensate for the losses. This, and the continuing laxity in ensuring proper assessment and collection of dues, has led to rapid deterioration in the financial status of public irrigation systems. The magnitude of losses—in relation to the full cost of the service provided—is now considerably larger than fresh investment in the sector. Another important contributing factor is the worsening fiscal health of states. Besides diverting resources from new investments to irrigation, infrastructure, and social services, this has contributed to the profligate and inefficient use of water, and a serious erosion of incentives for disciplined and prudent water management.

This trend was noted with concern by several official committees and, in particular, successive finance commissions. While emphasizing the necessity for improving cost recovery, they also progressively diluted the standards of cost recovery. Thus, the interest charges to be recovered from beneficiaries were lowered from 2.5 per cent of investment (recommended by the Fifth Finance Commission) to 1 per cent by the subsequent two commissions. Faced with the failure to meet even this target, the Eighth Commission chose to dilute it further, and exhorted states to ensure that at least the maintenance costs be recovered. The idea of recovering even part of the capital charges, recommended by several committees, was not accepted.

In the event, taking the country as a whole, revenues of both public irrigation works and state electricity boards were more or less adequate to cover operation and maintenance costs till the early 1970s. Thereafter, both capital costs and current operating costs have been rising rapidly, both for irrigation and electricity, because of domestic inflation in commodity prices, labour cost, and interest rates. These were compounded by laxity in the design and construction of projects, the choice of technology, and their continuing mismanagement. In the case of the state electricity boards (SEBs), an additional factor has been their increasing dependence on power purchased from non-ggovernmental utilities at relatively high prices. This, combined with the chronic failure to ensure that generating capacity increases in step with demand, has resulted in widespread incidence of unpredictable interruptions in supplies, voltage fluctuations, and outages. As with canal irrigation, the poor quality of service is a legitimate complaint of users.

State governments, however, have followed a deliberate policy of avoiding raising rates charged to farmers in step with costs. Canal rates have been revised infrequently, with great reluctance, and to a very limited extent. In the case of electricity, the rates have, in fact, been revised downwards, with many states announcing free power for agriculture. These policies are sought to be justified partly on the ground that the rise in input prices would reduce the returns to the use of key inputs, and dampen the pace of the adoption of new technology. Apprehensions of the adverse effects on the prospects of agricultural growth, and of the rapid reduction of rural poverty through the rapid rise in rural incomes and employment, are increasingly used to justify Government policy. These apprehensions are shared widely among professional economists. Insistent demands from the farm lobby for higher output prices, the opposition to raising input prices, and larger concerns about the slow pace of poverty reduction have strengthened the natural reluctance of the political class across all parties to address the problem.

The creation of highly differentiated rate structures has created strong incentives and huge opportunities for the under-assessment of dues. For instance, there are no water charges on wells within canal irrigation commands. Though such wells are fed mostly by the seepage of canal water, and farmers generally use both sources for the same field, they can avoid paying canal charges by getting it recorded as being irrigated by wells. Similarly, since water-intensive irrigated crops (like paddy and cane) carry much higher water rates, there is a strong inducement for the under-recording of the area under such crops with the collusion of local revenue/irrigation functionaries. There are strong reasons to believe that official statistics underestimate canal-irrigated areas, partly because they exclude illegal use of water (directly or indirectly) outside designated commands, and misclassify areas under conjunctive use under well irrigation. This leads to considerable under-assessment of water charges for canal irrigated areas. Data on irrigated areas actually using canal water are also unreliable. Revenue dues are also understated because of the under-reporting of areas under crops that carry high water charges. Their extent is, however, impossible to assess without more rigorous and careful field verification.

Electricity usage for lifting water for irrigation is not metered. Tampering of meters and laxity in ensuring that readings are taken regularly and accurately has always been a problem. With many states opting for the flat rate system—and many deciding to give free power to agriculture—the measurement of metered consumption has been given up. This makes it impossible to know how much power is used for strictly agricultural uses. It is now well established that statistics of agricultural use are notional and exaggerated: a high proportion of power reported to be consumed by agriculture—and a part of what is recorded as transmission and distribution losses—is, in fact, 'stolen' by illegal tapping and meter tampering. Besides encouraging theft through illegal pumping from rivers and canals, low electricity tariffs for agriculture have also led to the rapid growth of demand for groundwater pumping.

Moreover, as irrigation makes a huge difference to the yields and incomes of users, the temptation to vio-late rules, including illegal diversions, is strong. Actual collections are much less than assessed dues. Remissions on one ground or the other are frequent. Even making allowances for this, in a number of states the accumulated arrears add up to many times the actual annual collections. Laxity in assessment is compounded by laxity in collection. The Committee on the Pricing of Irrigation Water found that the actual revenue collection fell short of demand (that is, assessments) in a majority of states. Accumulated arrears—which do not include remissions and waivers granted by governments from time to time—were found to be nearly as large as the annual demand in some cases, and three to four times in many states. Governments pay little heed to these aspects: they are not even recognized as problems, let alone being assessed for their magnitude. On the contrary, they tend, for reasons of political expediency, not only to acquiesce in such violations but also to actually impede any attempt at checking them.

As a result, the gap between the cost of providing these inputs and realizations from ultimate users has grown manifold. Between 1990–1 and 2006–7, the magnitude of unrecovered costs on account of irrigation and electricity for agriculture has nearly trebled— from Rs 260 billion to Rs 750 billion. (Cumulated

TABLE 14   Unrecovered Costs on Account of Canal Irrigation and Electricity for Agriculture (Billion Rs at Current Prices)

Input	1990–1	1995–6	2000–1	2006–7
Irrigation	63	94	164	210
Power	155	247	206	281
Total	218	341	370	491

Source: The basis and methodology follow Srivatsava et al. (2003).

capital outlay, working expenses, and gross receipts are taken from CWC, *Water and Related Statistics 2004*. The interest on capital is taken at 10 per cent of cumulated capital outlay, which is closer to the actual average rate of interest on total government debt than assumed by the CWC. Depreciation is taken at 1 per cent). In the case of fertilizers, they are borne by the Central government, and shown explicitly in the budget. State governments bear the brunt of the deficit on account of electricity and irrigation; but only a part of it is provided explicitly in their budgets. Most of it is implicit, and difficult to trace under the existing practices of preparing and presenting accounts of government and its enterprises.

Unrecovered costs on agricultural inputs are a major factor in the governments' fiscal deficit, and cut into

resources available for investments augmenting productive capacity, and the extension and improvement
in the quality of social services (basic education and
health care, social security). In 1990–1, they accounted
for nearly half the gross fiscal deficit of Central and state
governments. Since then, this proportion has declined,
and is currently around 28 per cent. Moreover, unrecovered costs represent continuing, recurrent subventions
to those who are currently producing or consuming
these inputs. Again, despite an improvement in the ratio
of unrecovered costs to plan outlay (from 200 per cent
in 1990–1 to 88 per cent), unrecovered costs on water
and electricity alone are as large as the public sector plan
outlay on agriculture, rural development, and irrigation.
This shows how much they cut into the resources available for fresh investments. Improving cost recovery will,
thus, have significant beneficial effects, both on the
fisc and on the capacity to fund larger investments in
productive sectors, and for improving the coverage and
quality of social services.

Assumptions such as input prices need to be kept
low to make them affordable to farmers, higher input
prices will dampen incentives for their use, and outputs
are mostly dependent on the level of inputs used are

111

all questionable. The importance of efficiency of input management in cultivation needs far greater recognition and action than applies at present.

6

Inequalities in Access to Water

Access to water from rainfall or by utilizing renewable resources varies greatly across regions, uses, and users. The amount of naturally available water in any given location is limited by rainfall. Not all of it is available for use, partly because much of it is concentrated in a few months, and little is available in the dry season. Possibilities of mitigating this limitation by storing part of local rainfall, or by harnessing local streams, are also quite limited. In all these respects, there are large regional differences which are determined by nature and, therefore, not amenable to correction. On the contrary, there are concerns that climatic changes, the pace of economic development, and technological changes can cause major and unpredictable shifts in existing patterns.

The possibilities of augmentation as well as their magnitude are unevenly distributed. The extent to which surface water flows can be harnessed depends on harnessing flows generated in areas of high rainfall and during the monsoon season, and bringing them to downstream areas where populations and agriculture are concentrated. The volume of surface water flows varies across major river basins, and these are generally closely correlated to the level of rainfall they receive. The non-availability of suitable sites to store the surplus flows during the monsoon, international treaty obligations, and considerations of technical feasibility and economic viability, limit the extent to which they can be utilized.

It so happens that, across major basins, renewable and utilizable water resources follow similar patterns inter se, and in relation to total precipitation. This means that basins with higher rainfall and large surface flows also tend to have larger volumes that are utilizable. As for groundwater, the alluvial soils of the Indo-Gangetic Plains have deep aquifers that cover extensive areas, and can store huge volumes of water. This potential exists, though to a much smaller extent, in the flood plains and valleys of other major rivers. But over large parts of the country—particularly in the central Indian and the Deccan Plateau—aquiferous zones are shallower and highly fragmented. Their storage capacity is limited, and their replenishment rates are far more dependent on local rainfall and, therefore, very uneven across regions. However, areas that have the benefit of canal irrigation get additional recharge from seepage of surface water that can be reused.

Actual utilization relative to utilizable potential across regions is uneven because, for a variety of historical, technical, and political reasons, the pace of development has varied. The volume of water from man-made projects for various purposes, and the proportion of population and cultivated area benefiting from them are much higher as compared to rainfed areas. This is reflected in the fact that the area irrigated by them as a proportion of total cultivated area varies from negligible levels in some parts of the country, to nearly 100 per cent in many others.

These differences are reflected in the variations in the proportion of area and population that are benefiting, and the impact on the productivity of land across and within regions as well as within the area served by particular projects. These are different dimensions of the problem of unequal access to water between rainfed and irrigated areas, and of the distribution of the benefits of surface and groundwater development. They lie at the roots of the competition and conflict over water.

Tapping underground aquifers, and harnessing surface water from rivers that get water from a wider catchment, increases water supply to areas that benefit from them well above the availability for contiguous rainfed areas. The distribution of increased supply from the utilization of renewable supplies is also highly uneven between different uses and classes of users within states and river basins as well as within the command of particular projects. This, and the significant and widening differences between the productivity of rainfed and irrigated areas is one, and obviously important, aspect of unequal access.

Regional Distribution

The proportion of cultivated area that is irrigated by all sources currently ranges from less than 15 per cent in Odisha to over 90 per cent in the Punjab. Surface irrigation is more unevenly distributed than ground-water. The irrigation ratio, overall, as well as from surface and groundwater, has increased everywhere, though in different degrees. All have become more evenly diffused over time; this trend is more marked in groundwater than in surface irrigation. The pro-gressively wider diffusion of surface irrigation is due to the deliberate policy of the government; in the case of groundwater, the process is driven mostly by farmers themselves. Less uneven distribution of irri-gation across regions is driven entirely by farmers' decisions.

The process of expansion has brought out the grow-ing imbalance between the paces of growth in demand, relative to utilizable resources. Relative to population and cultivated area, utilizable surface water resources as well as the availability of suitable sites, their technical feasibility, and economic viability differ greatly across river basins. Faced with the clamour from farmers for the construction of projects, governments have taken up projects without strict attention to these factors. This clamour is manifest both in the intense disputes between riparian states over interstate rivers, and in pressures on states to take up numerous unauthorized, unapproved projects on such rivers.

Governments also respond to these pressures in deciding the extent of the area to be served by individual projects. Given the amount of water likely to be available in a particular reservoir, the area that can be irrigated depends on the cropping pattern in the command area. The area that can be irrigated will be larger when a larger proportion of the area is devoted to less water-intensive crops (such as sorghum and millets, pulses, and oilseeds) than when more water-intensive crops (like paddy, sugar cane, and vegetables) are grown. Projects tend to be designed on the assumption that cropping patterns will be restricted to the former pattern so that the project will serve as large an area and number of farmers as is possible with the available water. But, given the fact that water-intensive crop yields are far more remunerative to farmers, actual cropping patterns invariably turn out to be much more intensive than assumed in the design. These violations are supposed to attract severe penalties, but enforcing them is difficult, and strict enforcement is politically inexpedient. This is often cited as the reason why the

area actually irrigated turns out to be less than projected in the design.

Lax enforcement also leads to the illegal tapping of
water from the canals and reservoirs of the systems. It
also gives room—often with overt or tacit complicity
of the government—for more serious violations like
the illegal tapping of the water from the system for use
outside the command, and even more blatant ones like
the illegal pumping of water from rivers and streams,
the sand mining of riverbeds, and the pollution of
water bodies. These have major, and often disastrous,
consequences for both surface and groundwater availability along many rivers. Besides being iniquitous,
they also intensify water-related conflicts. But they
are seldom captured, or even sought to be captured, in
official data and policy pronouncements on water use
and irrigation.

Access to Different Classes

Access to water is also uneven between different classes
of farmers and different segments of the uses of water
for non-agricultural purposes. Taking the country as

a whole, National Sample Survey data show that the proportion of cultivated area irrigated is highest in holdings below 1 ha in size, and that this ratio declines progressively in larger-sized holdings. This is a consistent pattern over time, and apparent both in respect of all sources, and also for surface and groundwater. The inverse relation between holding size and irrigation ratio, however, shows a progressive weakening over time. Thus, at the national level, the overall irrigation ratio in holdings with less than 1 ha was about four times the ratio in holdings with more than 10 ha in the early 1950s; by the early 1990s it was only one-and-a-half times. While the extent of irrigated area, both in absolute terms and as a proportion of area cultivated, has grown in all size classes, it has increased much less in smaller-sized holdings than in larger ones. This national-level pattern may be partly a reflection of the more rapid expansion of irrigation facilities in some regions—mainly in regions of relatively low rainfall where holdings are larger than the national average. Nevertheless, there is a widespread feeling that the growth of irrigation facilities and the way they are managed are biased against small and marginal farmers.

In the case of surface irrigation, in any given region, the distribution of landholdings in command areas is unlikely to be different from non-command areas; nor is there likely to be much of a difference between different segments of the command area. Such advantages that lands closer to canals and distributaries may have in accessing water cannot have any systematic bias in favour of larger farmers. However, inequity can arise, and favour cultivators with larger holdings to the extent they have the influence and clout to get away with the violation of rules of access and use, and/or the ability to influence the scheduling and delivery of water to meet their requirements. This advantage is likely to be much greater in the case of groundwater for two reasons. The first is the capacity to invest in wells, tube wells, and pump sets is clearly greater for larger farmers. This is especially so in the context of falling water tables, declining water yields, and larger costs involved in deepening wells and installing more powerful pumps. The second is the development of water markets permitting small farmers without wells—or those experiencing reduced supplies from their wells—buying water from larger farmers with surplus water. However, all available evidence suggests that these markets are thin, and supplies available for sale are highly volatile. Small farmers are clearly at a disadvantage in such a situation. How extensively and seriously they are affected by this disadvantage needs closer and more systematic study.

Rainfed Lands

A combination of poor-quality degraded soils, and inadequate and uncertain moisture are the basic constraints that account for the productivity of rainfed lands being much below that of irrigated crops. This inherent disadvantage has been compounded by deterioration of their soils, reduction in their capacity to make effective use of local rainfall, and lack of techniques for improvement in yields of rainfed crops. As a result, productivity of unirrigated lands has increased, if at all, much more slowly than in the case of irrigated crops, thereby widening the disparities between them.

The importance of soil and moisture conservation, and research on dry farming has long been recognized. Pioneering work was done, especially in the erstwhile Bombay Presidency, since the 1930s, and has continued to figure in post-Independence agricultural develop-ment strategy. However, the construction of large stor-ages, and encouraging groundwater exploitation for irrigation came to be viewed as being more critical in raising productivity in agriculture. In contrast, the interest and effort put into soil and moisture conser-vation programmes was, at best, lukewarm, and their implementation was quite indifferent. Allocations were, of course, small compared to what was spent on irriga-tion, but not insubstantial. Special irrigation projects for drought-prone and desert areas were given priority and launched. But they did not result in any significant and lasting improvement of rainfed agriculture.

The reason is that interventions through contour bunding, trenching, and other measures on individual farmers' fields are not effective in preventing erosion, and improving the capacity of soils to absorb rainwater and retain moisture. They have to be accompanied by measures to check runoff through natural drainage channels, many of which are part of government or village common lands. The appropriate unit for such interventions is the watershed, starting at the village level. This is necessary to make it possible to trap as much of local precipitation as possible for use within the village. This requires institutional arrangements that can prepare and implement a soil and moisture conservation plan for the watershed as a whole, and ensure that they are kept in good repair.

A part of the increased availability of water gets stored in the soil, a part can be impounded in small local ponds, and a part helps increase recharge in local aquifers. Also, the augmentation of water supply to raise the overall productivity of crops and useful biomass from common lands cannot be left entirely to individuals; it has to be decided at the community level. It is this understanding that underlies the concept of integrated watershed development that came into prominence during the late 1960s and 1970s, and got accepted as the core strategy for rainfed areas.

This was a significant and welcome break from traditional approaches to improving water availability in rainfed areas. The coverage of integrated watershed development programmes has grown, and now extends to the whole country. So has the scale of outlays. But the institutional arrangements and the way they function leave much to be desired. The planning and implementation of the programmes is wholly the responsibility of the states. Guidelines as to how these functions are to be handled emphasize the importance of integrated planning, the coordination between different line departments at the ground level, consultation with beneficiary groups through village watershed committees, and the need to decide the works to be done keeping in view specific local conditions.

In reality, the various components of watershed development are decided and implemented by different line departments acting more or less independently, and without taking local conditions into account. Monitoring by higher-level state officials is weak. There is no arrangement for the independent audit of performance and impact. Watershed committees are not always constituted; their membership is not representative of different interest groups; and they are not involved—or even consulted seriously—in making decisions or in overseeing their implementation. That the entire cost met by government funds is hardly conducive to local communities acquiring a sense of ownership of the programmes. And yet, they are expected to take over the responsibility for the continued maintenance of the works, evolve criteria for sharing such extra water as become available, and the resultant increase in useful biomass between different beneficiary groups, and ensure that they are observed.

These deficiencies, and the needed reforms, have been reviewed by many official committees, NGOs actively involved in the programmes, and independent scholars. They have emphasized the need to consolidate all soil and water conservation programmes for dry-lands into a single unified watershed programme and decentralize its planning and implementation down to the ground level. Village panchayats should be given the central role in planning and implementation, with technical advice and help from NGOs and government agencies. While the scale of financial allocations has increased manifold, the creation of the National Rainfed Area Development Authority—with powers to lay down guidelines on the scope and content of the programmes and financial allocations—has had the effect of centralizing it. The programmes continue to suffer from fragmented planning and implementation, the non-involvement of beneficiary communities, and the lack of local institutions for deciding and enforcing rules regarding the maintenance of facilities and shar-ing costs/benefits within the community.

That the panchayats are not currently equipped to handle the responsibility is the alibi for opposing decentralization. Addressing this lacuna is, of course, difficult and challenging. The experience of many NGO initiatives shows that the problem is not insoluble, but requires patient and sustained effort. The real hurdle is state opposition to decentralization that empowers elected local bodies. The political class in most states is actively opposed to transferring authority, responsibility, and resources to panchayats. The large amount of soft money provided through central assistance, and the weak mechanisms for the scrutiny of spending and auditing of projects leaves ample room for those in power to use the funds to promote their political interests, and for outright corruption.

7

Conflicts over Water

The demand for irrigation has increased apace because it increases land productivity, and also because the pricing policies for inputs and outputs increases the returns to irrigated agriculture (especially cultivation using groundwater) relative to rainfed lands. The demand for non-agricultural uses of water has grown even more rapidly because of population growth, increase in per capita income, urbanization, and industrialization. The expansion in the supply of surface and groundwater has not kept pace with the growth of demand for water from all users. This has led to competition, conflict, and social tension over access to and use of available water between different uses and users at all levels.

Managing Conflicts

Managing water conflicts calls for attention to certain special features of this resource. The extraction and use of water in any one part of a system (river basin or sub-basin, reservoir command or aquifers) has significant effects on other parts of the system; and the scope for mutual interference in usage is pervasive. For instance, the impoundment of flow upstream of a river/stream reduces flow available for use downstream within a given river basin or sub-basin. The water available to tailenders of a canal depends to a significant extent on extraction by the head and middle reaches. Increased pumping by some affects supply to others. The deepening of wells depending on the same aquifer by some reduces supplies to others, forcing the latter also to dig deeper.

Partly for this reason, and also because the utility of water depends on how much and when it is available at specific locations, it is impossible to define enforceable property rights to individual users which can be traded with other users through the market mechanism. The difficulties are compounded when the number of users/

claimants is large. In any case, being a critical natural resource, it is essential to ensure that the distribution of access and use of water to different claimants is socially equitable—and also sustainable—over the long term. These considerations rule out privatization and leaving allocations to the market mechanism.

The USA is often cited as a successful instance of allowing users traceable private rights over water. However, most large public systems have been constructed by governments and managed by public authorities. In the western parts of the country— where many irrigation systems have historically been developed by private parties—traceable rights are recognized; but they are in the nature of entitlements to use, and do not amount to ownership. It is important to note that the rights and obligations of users, both within individual systems and between different systems on the same river, are clearly articulated. Institutional arrangements at each level have mechanisms to enforce them. And disputes over them are justiciable in courts.

Clearly, the American system and those modelled on it can hardly be considered as market-mediated management of water allocation. While private user rights and their tradability are recognized, they are subject to clear rules monitored and enforced by strong and functioning autonomous institutions at the system level and higher-level public institutions, the government, and law courts. As available resources for traditional uses (mainly agriculture) are getting more or less fully exhausted, and demand for non-agricultural uses is increasing, trading in user rights has increased. With urban water supply organizations seeking to meet their growing needs by buying water from prior right holders, transfers of rights are taking place but, by all accounts, only on a limited scale. Transfers for agricultural use across different systems in a basin, or even within a particular system, seem quite limited. Reduced agricultural demand for water, the huge size of farms, and the relatively small number of rights holders have allowed this process to work. However, the process is neither extensive nor smooth and conflict-free. It is subject to approval through the judicial process.

Conditions in India are very different; the government plays a dominant role in deciding access to and the use of water resources based on the concept that the state is the ultimate owner of this resource. However, this right is exercised only in the case of surface water. It is exercised through laws which prohibit private and non-governmental entities from divert-ing or impounding water flows in all surface streams without government approval. Nearly all large surface works are constructed by state governments which decide which projects are to be taken up within their boundaries, who is entitled to the use of water and for what purpose, and makes laws and regulations for their management. Regulation of groundwater use is very weak, leaving it more or less free to be exploited by the private sector.

The Indian Situation

The principles of sharing water of interstate rivers between riparian states and between different segments of river basins and sub-basins within each state are not clearly defined. Nor are the institutional mecha-nisms to ensure that they are applied consistently and enforced effectively. Ideally, basin plans as well as plans for individual projects should aim at the optimal use of available water from all sources that ensures maxi-mum sustainable benefit for the region as a whole. But this is seldom attempted: the task is too complex to be resolved purely on an objective basis. In any case, the current state of knowledge, analytical techniques, and empirical data is wholly inadequate to handle it. Entitlements are defined in terms of the volume of water that riparian states of interstate basins can use.

Entitlements to the waters of the Krishna, Godavari, and Narmada basins were decided by special tribunals in the 1960s and the 1970s. Their awards are accepted as binding. For other interstate rivers, the CWC estimated utilizable flows in each state. These are judgments based on estimates of the flows generated, the possibilities of utilization, and the requirements of agriculture and other uses for the population in each of their regions. The tribunal judgments and pre-existing agreements on sharing of the Kaveri waters (and some other rivers) are due for review. Moreover, over time, the basis and fairness of the existing patterns of sharing are being questioned. Faced with widespread and intense grassroots pressures for projects to augment water supply—especially in water-short and backward regions—the standards of scrutiny of projects on interstate rivers which require the Centre's approval have greatly weakened. Increasingly, states have been taking up projects without even seeking central clearance. The Centre has been reluctant to exercise its powers under the Interstate Water Disputes Act to initiate dispute resolution mechanisms. Tribunal proceedings are long-drawn-out, and decisions take an inordinate amount of time. In any case, they are increasingly contested in courts of the higher judiciary without definitive and binding judgments.

In the case of surface projects meant mainly for irrigation, all farmers with land in the command area are, in principle, entitled to get water on certain conditions regarding permissible cropping patterns. Communities within the command are also permitted to use the water for local non-agricultural purposes. Individual users of irrigation systems are defined in terms of the area for which they can get water. Individual entitlements are not specified for those who use it for non-agricultural purposes. Entitlements in terms of area may be lost when, as often happens, the effective command area turns out to be less than promised or water is used in violation of rules or by those with no rights. The content of entitlements in terms of quantum, duration, and timing of supplies to individual users is seldom specified. Nor are the entitlements legally enforceable. In any case, government is free to change entitlements by expanding the command area, modifying schedules, and diverting water to other uses. Decisions on all these aspects are made and changed by the government and its bureaucracy without any consultation with the beneficiaries.

Violation of rules of water allocation and use in public systems and unauthorized and illegal appropriation of water for agriculture as well as non-agricultural uses are rampant. Given the fuzziness of entitlements and the huge number of users and plots in canal commands, monitoring and enforcement of rules is impossible. Neither are there any credible institutional mechanisms for the redressal of grievances over the denial of entitlements. Penalties for violations are rarely enforced. The more powerful use their influence with the political class and the bureaucracy to change rules in their favour, or to condone their violations. The grievances of the less privileged hardly get attention. Conflicts are invariably settled by the balance of local power and influence in user communities. Litigation is rarely resorted to since the process is far too tedious and costly, and the outcome uncertain.

In the case of groundwater, the law gives all land-holders the right to extract as much water as they can from under their land, subject to their not adversely affecting the ability of others to exercise the same right. Establishing the latter being extremely difficult, courts do not provide a satisfactory mechanism for settling disputes. The government has the power to regulate the exploitation of groundwater by imposing conditions regarding spacing between wells and their deepening, and enforce them by withholding power connections. Such regulations exist on paper, but are not enforceable in the face of the surging demand for wells and tube wells from a huge number of farmers.

Over time, as the volume of water pumped has begun to exceed the water available from dug wells, the process of deepening and the installation of more powerful pumps has gathered pace. This has called for investments of a magnitude which cannot be afforded by all farmers. Small and marginal farmers have had to be content with lower yields from their wells and, in extreme cases, abandon those that have dried up. The emergence of water markets has helped small cultivators, but only to a limited extent. The legal right of individuals to extract groundwater, subject to the condition that it must not adversely affect availability for other users, is virtually ineffective. Recourse to courts to enforce this right is too costly and prone to delays, and outcomes are uncertain. They are only of theoretical interest when, in the absence of any regulation of groundwater extraction and use, competitive deepening of wells and tube wells is widespread and growing. Farmers of small means who seek to invest, often by borrowing, in deepening their existing wells or constructing new ones in the hope of striking it rich, face high risks of failure. This has often made the debt burden unbearable, an important cause of farmer suicides.

The growing urban demand is sought to be met essentially by augmenting supply. As local sources are exhausted, state governments resort to pumping of groundwater to feed public systems from aquifers (including riverbeds) that are already under stress, diverting water from irrigation works, in many cases over long distances, thereby reducing supplies to agriculture uses and through special water supply projects to store or divert rivers whose water are already under contestation among existing users. This is a source of increasing agricultural/non-agricultural and rural/urban conflict.

Environmental Concerns

If water management is a functioning anarchy, the handling of other concerns over water resource development and use—submergence and displacement, the environmental impact of large reservoirs, groundwater depletion and water pollution—also leaves much to be desired.

Overuse and misuse of water, fertilizers, and pesticides in irrigated areas, increasing depths from which groundwater is extracted, and discharge of large quantities of untreated urban sewage and industrial effluents has resulted in increasingly widespread pollution of both surface and groundwater sources. Large stretches of most rivers and many natural/man-made storage water bodies have been polluted. In many regions, these waters have become unfit for human consumption, agriculture, and fishery. According to official statistics (www.wrmin.nic.in), 70 districts have been affected by salinity and contamination by fluorides and heavy metals, 95 by nitrates, and seven by arsenic. Independent assessments by non-governmental agencies suggest that the incidence is more widespread and serious.

The construction of large reservoirs involves the submergence of considerable extents of land, (including forests, some of which are havens of biodiversity), the displacement of a large number of people residing in the submerged areas, and damage to downstream estuarine ecosystems. Reliable data on the magnitude of different effects are lacking. According to one estimate (World Bank 1991), the area submerged by reservoirs is between 3 per cent and 8 per cent of their command area, a sizeable part consisting of forests. The distribution network takes up another 2 to 5 per cent of land (much of it already under cultivation). Estimates of the number of persons displaced by dams vary widely: some estimates place it at 20 million to 40 million, which is much higher than official figures. While these estimates are yet to be properly assessed, there is no doubt that the impact is much larger and wider than officials admit. Also obvious is that these have long been neglected in water resource planning.

A sizeable and growing irrigated area is affected by waterlogging and salinity due to over-irrigation, rising water tables, and neglect of drainage. Rough estimates suggest that about 5 per cent of the area under irrigation commands is affected by salinity and as much as a fifth is waterlogged. There is much concern for the impact of storages and diversions of rivers in reducing river flows well below minimum regime levels, and the consequent damage and destruction of fish and other forms of aquatic, animal, and plant species in downstream areas, and of marshes in the estuaries that play an important role as breeding grounds for fish and maintaining a healthy coastal ecology.

Growing public awareness of these issues and the serious consequences of neglecting them have prompted some tightening of procedures. Terms for land acquisition as well as compensation for project displaced persons for loss of livelihood and measures for their rehabilitation, and environmental impact assessment and measures to minimize adverse consequences as a condition for the clearance of projects have been made mandatory. Industrial users have been made responsible for ensuring that they do not discharge untreated effluents into surface and groundwater sources, and take appropriate measures to this end at their cost with penalties for non-compliance. A separate Ministry of Environment has been created at the Centre, and most states have set up separate agencies dealing with environmental and pollution problems. Of late, the central ministry has been insisting that an expert assessment of the ecological impact of large-scale water projects be submitted, making environmental clearances essential before approval for implementation. This activism has evoked strong opposition from both public and private investors (and their potential beneficiaries) on the ground that it has become the source of inordinate delays for many important projects.

Action to prevent and check these unhealthy trends and measures to correct them are patchy and incomplete in coverage, and implementation is widely criticized for being indifferent and tardy. Mechanisms for the redressal of grievances are notoriously ineffective. The data relevant for the assessment of the environment leave much to be desired in terms of both coverage and quality. The responsibility for verifying specific complaints of violation, enforcing penalties, and getting violators to take corrective action rests entirely with the states. Both the central and state governments have been—and still are—reluctant to address these tasks in spite of widespread agitations by civil society groups on the extensive violations of environment laws and the resulting damage to water bodies and the livelihood and health of innumerable people.

Innumerable complaints of violation have been, and are, being brought before the courts for adjudication. The standards of evidence needed to establish the fact of damage and its extent beyond reasonable doubt turn out to be difficult.

Polluters invariably contest the facts and inferences regarding the adverse impacts they are accused of. Ambivalence in the law works in their favour. Moreover, they have both the resources and the stamina to go through prolonged litigation. Despite this, there are numerous instances where the courts have ruled that those adversely affected by pollution are entitled to compensation, have ordered polluters to take corrective measures, and have upheld the principle of polluter pays. In most cases, the enforcement of the award is left to state governments which have been both unwilling and unable to do so because of the political clout of the owners of polluting industries, reinforced by the threat of large-scale layoff of their workers.

Over the years, as the displaced have become more conscious of their rights, dissatisfaction with the terms of rehabilitation and resettlement and the failure to implement them has led to extensive litigation and mass agitations. In numerous cases referred to courts, judgments have insisted on fulfilling terms of compensation announced at the time of acquisition, or have awarded more liberal terms. But governments have been recalcitrant in implementing the judgments and courts have been helpless in enforcing strict and complete compliance.

There are sharp divisions in society over the extent to which the needs of rapid economic development are in conflict with protecting the environment. Credible measures call for far more stringent standards of project scrutiny, for governments to minimize the potential long-term damage to the economy and society, or accept slower growth in the medium term. The real difficulty lies in the unwillingness of both individual enterprises and users of services to pay additional costs. And, neither is the citizenry at large prepared to bear them through additional taxation.

In sum, the state of water resources development and management in the country is unsatisfactory. It is also apparent that the deficiencies in the way water resource development programmes are formulated, approved, and implemented are persistent, even becoming more pronounced. Public awareness of these adverse environmental and social impacts of water resource development has no doubt increased. Concerns about the persistence of these trends have been documented in numerous research and evaluation studies by scholars, and articulated by activists through various public forums, agitations, and in courts of law.

Growing awareness of the importance of improving water-use efficiency, watershed development among planners and policymakers, and the initiatives being taken to address the problem, are encouraging signs. Some states have, no doubt, brought about major changes in the management of surface water systems to improve water-use efficiency by giving priority to the maintenance of distribution networks, the collection of water charges at the tertiary level, and participation in the management of systems at all levels. The Planning Commission is making a serious effort to correct excessive preoccupation with construction of new projects by giving greater importance and resources to the modernization of old systems, minor works projects, speedier completion of projects; improving water-use efficiency; and integrated watershed development. But these initiatives have to be taken much further and become more central to the development strategy.

But water resource departments of both the Centre and the states continue to believe that massive programmes to augment water supplies are essential to meet the requirements of a rapidly growing and increasingly prosperous economy. There is strong political and bureaucratic resistance to radical decentralization of water management to user-controlled organizations. Industries are unwilling to accept obligations for control and abatement of pollution or to bear the costs involved. They are also opposed to the enforcement of strict environmental conditions on water resource projects, not on the ground that they are unnecessary, but because they would greatly increase the cost of the projects and therefore make them unviable. Attempts to raise water rates, so essential to induce more efficient use of water, are frustrated by fierce opposition from users and from the political class. Unwilling to confront the political challenge to these measures, they are a strong lobby for large-scale inter-basin transfers of surface flows and artificial recharge.

8

Solutions for Effective Water Management

Limits to Augmentation

The case for a continued emphasis on the augmentation of water supply is based on long-term projections showing that the growing requirements for domestic, agricultural, and non-agricultural uses cannot be met unless the pace of exploitation of utilizable potential is accelerated. It is argued that even if this were to be done, the utilizable potential would fall short of requirements within the next 15 years, and that this gap would widen further thereafter. Therefore, it is necessary to explore ways to augment the utilizable potential through inter-basin transfers.

In the year 2000, agriculture is estimated to have used 540 bcm of water (mostly for irrigation); usage for non-agricultural purposes was placed at a little over 90 bcm; and the total usage for all purposes at 630 bcm. The water requirements of agriculture are projected to increase to 900 bcm in 2025, and become close to 1,100 bcm in 2050. These estimates are based on certain assumptions about the growth of population and per capita incomes, the resulting growth in the demand for food and fibre, and the increase in irrigated area required to produce the needed output. Requirements for non-agricultural uses are expected to grow even more rapidly because of the rapid growth of industries, power generation, and demand for water for domestic and other non-agricultural uses. These are projected to touch 180 bcm in 2025 and 370 bcm by 2050. On this basis, total requirements of surface and groundwater are expected to increase from 630 bcm in 2000 to 1,080 bcm in 2025, and 1,450 bcm by 2050.

According to this argument, the total utilizable potential of surface and groundwater in the country is, as assessed at 1,100 bcm to 1,200 bcm by the CWC, is just about equal to the projected requirements in

2025, and well short of requirements in 2050. Hence, the need to ensure that measures are taken to exploit all utilizable potential in the next two decades. Moreover, exploring the possibilities of augmenting utilizable water through large-scale inter-basin transfers to meet the growing gap between requirements and availability is an urgent need.

Questionable Inferences

However, the basis of the above projections and the inferences derived from them are questionable on many grounds.

• The projections for irrigation water requirements are based on the expected growth in demand for food grains generated by certain assumptions about the growth of population and incomes, and of judgments of (a) the extent of increase in cropping intensity and yields under irrigated and rainfed conditions; and (b) the extent of irrigated area required to increase food grain production to meet this demand. (c) Projections for non-agricultural uses are based on assumptions on population growth, urbanization, norms of desirable levels of supply for domestic use, assumptions (based on rather patchy data) of average use of water per unit of output, projected output levels in different industries, and for power generation.

- Increases in crop intensity and yields depend not only on the extent of irrigated area but also on cropping pattern changes, improvements in bio-chemical technology for crops, and how well they are managed. All these are interrelated in complex ways which are far from well understood, and which are also variable across crops and regions. Projections of irrigated area and irrigation water requirements without a critical examination of these aspects for the country as a whole cannot be considered definitive. Projections for non-agricultural uses are even more so.

- The estimates of water requirements relate to gross utilization for various purposes. Effective usage is much less. A rough estimate—based on ET rates of different irrigated crops in different regions—of the overall consumptive use of water from rainfall and irrigation is around 550 mm per ha, of which 260 mm is from rainfall and irrigation contributes 290 mm. Assuming, as the long-term projections of desirable irrigated areas seem to do, that gross irrigated area has to be doubled from 80 mha in 2000 to 160 mha in 2050, the total consumptive use of water to be met from irrigation sources will increase from 240 bcm to 480 bcm over this period. Including non-agricultural uses, the total require-ments for consumptive use for all purposes will increase from 250 bcm to 520 bcm.

• Though not so easy to achieve, this is far less than the projections of gross irrigation water requirements suggest. In agriculture, as much as two-thirds of gross supplies are lost through seepage and evapora-tion in the process of conveyance and application, and for non-consumptive uses. The magnitude of these losses is variable across different sources: losses are much less in the case of groundwater than in surface systems. They also vary across regions. As already noted, rough estimates suggest that, across major river basins, the ratio of effective use to gross utilization in irrigation varies from 27 or 28 per cent to 55 per cent. System-level data, though dated and limited to some 150 systems, suggest that this ratio ranges between 10 per cent and 90 per cent. The ratio of effective to gross use in the case of domestic and industrial purposes is even lower: most (as much as 90 per cent in many cases) of such water used goes back to streams, rivers, and underground storage as effluent, and is available for reuse. If allowance is made for reducing these losses and for greater recycling of waste water, the gross requirements will grow much slower than requirements for effective use.

• If, as current estimates suggest, the untilized potential of groundwater is much larger than that of surface water, and the share of groundwater increases, the overall ratio of net to gross use will increase. There is clearly much scope for increasing effective utilization rates and the careful use of water on the field in surface irrigation systems as well as for recycling waste water in all uses. If the overall ratio of net to gross uses can be increased from the present 30 per cent to 33 per cent by 2025, and to 40 per cent by 2050, the required gross volume of supply for all uses will be 660 bcm and 1,000 bcm, respectively in these two years. This is well within the current estimates of 1,100–1,200 bcm as the utilizable water potential for the country. The hype about the necessity for inter-basin transfers through interlinking of rivers is unjustified. However, there is no doubt that the expansion of water supplies to 1,000 bcm, and increasing utilization efficiency to 40 per cent by 2050 presents a difficult challenge.

- Currently, completed surface projects are estimated to have a live storage capacity of 190 bcm. Ongoing projects (76 of them) are estimated to add another 107 bcm to storage capacity. Together, they will supply an estimated 500 bcm of water on average. The pace of implementation of these projects has been extremely tardy despite the high priority given to their speedy completion, and their being backed by massive fund allocations. It remains to be seen whether the Planning Commission will succeed in ensuring that the allocations are, in fact, used for completing projects according to the prioritization, within the revised estimates of costs, and the targeted time frame of about a decade.

- This leaves some 130 projects with a storage capacity of 108 bcm, the completion of which will, it is said, see the full utilization of surface water potential (690 bcm). They include many large—some very large—storages, mostly in the sub-Himalayan regions. Apart from the fact that the necessary preparatory investigations (much less the technical aspects of design) have not been done in sufficient detail, many of the dam sites are on international rivers requiring agreements with other riparian nations. These negotiations have been going on for a long time: no consensus has been arrived at regarding the sharing of waters, much less formal treaties signed. Moreover, these are located on more difficult sites—in ecologically fragile and highly seismic regions. Apart from the high risks of damage to reservoirs under these conditions, and their environmental implications, the costs are likely to be much higher than the sites of existing and ongoing projects. The effect of all these on the economic viability of investments is yet to be examined and assessed. Given all this, the prospects of these projects being taken up in the next decade, and their commissioning within the next two or three decades, are quite dim.

- Technical feasibility is not the sole basis for assessing utilizable supplies; economic viability, judged by likely returns in terms of additional output, and

153

other benefits relative to costs, are equally important. The lack of adequate and reliable data on these aspects is a major problem even in respect of existing projects. Anticipating them in respect of new ones is even more problematic. Nevertheless, certain general observations can be made with confidence. The costs of constructing reservoirs, pumping water, and distribution networks are a function of the characteristics of storage sites (terrain, geology, seismic hazards), and the distance between the storage and the location where water is to be used will depend on the sophistication of distribution systems. Easier and less costly sites have been already exploited, new ones—many of them in areas of high seismic activity—pose greater difficulties and, therefore, entail greater expense. Costs will, therefore, increase.

• These considerations apply with greater force to inter-basin transfers which some see as the way to redress the uneven distribution of water across basins. Apart from environmental and related concerns—which apply to these as much, perhaps more than, they do to the usual storage projects—their feasibility is very much in question. The stark fact is that most rivers in the country have peak flows during roughly the same season, namely the monsoon. Diversion of surplus flows during this season to feed dry regions, and in the dry season, involves crossing formidable natural barriers, and finding sites for storing immense amounts of water.

- Many doubt whether the magnitude of surpluses will allow for transfer to water-short, low rainfall regions (and uplands) in quantities and at times that would make a significant difference. The estimated costs involved are not only beyond the resources available to the government, but are unconscionably large in relation to the projected increase in supplies, and relative to other important claims on public funds.

- Despite all this, some national political parties and parties in water-short regions (for example Tamil Nadu) are actively campaigning for it. With the blessings and prodding of the Supreme Court, the subject is now a live public issue. Detailed technical assessments and difficulties in getting the states concerned—and farmers in the so-called 'surplus' basins—to agree to the transfers are being much discussed. Enforcing the agreements may well stall the programme, but at the heavy price of distracting

155

the attention of the public, the politicians, and the government from the more important and urgent tasks of improving the efficiency of water management.

• There are concerns that, in many areas, groundwater exploitation is exceeding the natural rates of recharge, calling for measures to contain the level of extraction within sustainable limits. However, of the assessed utilizable groundwater potential of 420 bcm, only one-fourths is estimated to be currently utilized. It is recognized that these estimates need to be systematically validated through aquifer mapping, and surveys of actual water extraction from all wells and tube wells used for irrigation and for non-agricultural purposes. A reassessment of these aspects and the possibilities of artificial recharge—now being taken up seriously—would provide the basis for a more confident estimate of the potential and its spatial distribution. There is also need for a better idea of recharge and utilization in surface system commands to assess the scope for more extensive conjunctive use. The pace and extent of exploitation of these potentials will largely depend on firmer assessments of costs and returns.

Improving Efficiency in
Water Distribution

Given the uncertainties regarding the pace and extent of increase in utilized volumes of both surface and groundwater, measures to increase the efficiency of water use have acquired urgency. Improvements in the technical efficiency of water use as well as recycling can substantially reduce the volume of freshwater needed to meet a given level of consumptive use. There is also considerable room for improving the efficiency at the users' end: the adoption of conservation measures, the better management of water to ensure that supplies are adjusted to the needs of end-users, and water management at the system and farm levels so that the soil moisture regime is conducive to realizing the full yield potential of existing and improved biochemical technology. This is well recognized in professional discourses on water policy, and even in the rhetoric of government policy pronouncements. However, they are not given due importance in planning and resource allocation. Improving water-use efficiency calls for a substantial shift in investment priorities away from new constructions to improving physical facilities and control structures in existing systems. This would result in better-regulated distribution and could be combined with institutional changes to improve water management as well as strong economic incentives to induce users to adopt water-saving practices.

A large number of existing surface systems are over a hundred years old. The physical structure of their headworks, their canals, distribution networks, and drainage facilities are in a bad state. Even in more recent systems, these networks are inadequate to ensure the smooth flow of water to all sections of the command. Apart from this, there are no regulatory devices for monitoring and regulating water deliveries to different segments of the command in a flexible manner. The modernization of systems is called for, and this requires large investments.

During the last decade, such programmes have been accorded greater prominence in five-year plans. Further increases are envisaged in the future. However, the scale and scope envisaged by the programmes are inadequate. Much larger outlays are necessary. At present, modernization programmes tend to focus mainly on civil engineering works, repairing damage, and improving alignments/gradients to restore capacity.

More attention needs to be given to installing modern regulatory devices at all strategic points, including at tertiary levels. The quality of preparatory technical and engineering studies needs to be greatly improved to ensure the sound designing and choice of appropriate mixes suited to the specific conditions of different projects. Moreover, hardly any attention is given to assessing the magnitude of increase in actual water supply at the field level over current level. Also essential is a systematic study to assess the present sources and extent of losses, and how much of proposed physical improvement in the system should be made mandatory. An objective ex post facto assessment should also be made of the actual increase achieved after the completion of the project to judge its success.

Equally important is making sure that physical structures and equipment are kept in good working condition. The neglect of maintenance by system managers (due to inadequate staff and funding) has been the main reason for the deterioration in systems. Farmers have little role or stake in the process. The decentralization of the responsibility for regular maintenance and repair to user associations is essential. In this respect, the experience of Andhra Pradesh shows that empowering and enabling user associations to take over this task is feasible, effective, and economical.

Increasing Productivity per Unit of Water

The increased availability of water resulting from system improvement and its modernization will, no doubt, contribute to increasing production. But, increasing output per unit of water used by crops is far more difficult. In order to get the most output per unit of consumptive use from available biochemical technology, it is necessary to ensure that soil moisture conditions are maintained at optimum levels in different segments of the command. This optimum varies between crops and seasons, depending both on natural rainfall and the ability to adjust the quantum and timing of irrigation supplies according to the condition of the crops being grown in specific locations. This requires (i) a distribution system equipped with devices for a flexible regulation of water deliveries to different sections of the command; (ii) the continuous monitoring of soil moisture status, especially during the critical phases of the growth of different crops being raised in different parts of the command; and (iii) the ability of system managers to adapt the scheduling of water distribution based on this information in each season. Given all these, the realization of the full potential of available biochemical technology will depend on the quality of water management in specific fields as well as the agronomic practices used by individual farmers.

This ideal is difficult to realize under existing conditions. For one, we need to know what the optimum soil moisture regime should be under different agro-climatic conditions for different crops, the actual regimes under actual rainfall and irrigation on soil moisture status at the field level in different systems, and the yield response to different levels and combinations of biochemical inputs. Knowledge regarding these relations is generally inadequate, despite the considerable number of controlled experiments conducted in research stations during the 1970s and 1980s. Not only have the resulting data not been analysed but the experiments themselves have been discontinued.

Farmers depending entirely on groundwater and, to a lesser extent, when using it in conjunction with surface water, can use their first-hand observation of the condition of the crops to decide when a particular crop is under stress, what the critical phases are, and accordingly decide when and how much water to apply from their wells. This is difficult in surface systems, since individual farmers have no control over when and how much water they will get. Given the uncertainties of canal supply, and the very low effective cost of water, they have neither the incentive nor the ability to manage the available supplies to their maximum advantage. The task of ensuring reliable and timely supplies to all users is also very difficult for system managers.

Surface systems serve large areas, and a huge number of plots growing numerous crops dispersed in unevenly distributed patches. Even at the time of designing, assumptions regarding cropping patterns within different sections of the ayacut are not specified in any detail. The water requirements of crops are based on the area which can be irrigated per unit volume of overall water supply from the system. Scheduling rules are based on conditions in a normal year, and ensuring that they match the spatial distribution of the area of different crops and seasons is extremely difficult. That this is not attempted is not surprising. But, the operation of these rules changes, from year to year, and season to season, in the light of actual cropping patterns, inflows into the reservoir, and rainfall conditions. Hardly any project manager prepares a water budget based on proper measurements of the sources and uses of water, efficiency of use, and productivity. System managers tend to view their role in rather narrow terms—as one of delivering water according to the rules specified in operational manuals and government orders rather than striving for optimum impact on yields.

Besides improvement in physical infrastructure, better-designed and strictly enforced rules of scheduling of supplies—all of which require major changes in the organization and management of surface works—will increase predictability of supplies at the farm level. However, the problem of regulating supplies to enable individual farmers to maintain optimal soil moisture conditions in their fields will remain.

The task can be made more manageable by shifting from the present system of direct delivery to individual plots to an arrangement under which the system agrees to provide water to user associations at the outlet level. A contract specifying the volume and timing of water to be supplied, the payment to be made by the association to the system, and the responsibilities of the association for the regular maintenance and repair of distribution channels serving them would be in order. The contract would also specify penalties that either party would have to pay for non-observance. User associations can be left free to decide how the water supply and costs of local maintenance are to be shared among their members. This will reduce to manageable dimensions the system functionaries' task of monitoring distribution and use. Given the commitment on the quantity and timing of supply to associations, there is no need for the system to have any rules on permissible cropping patterns. The associations can decide what crops are to be grown with the system supply, and be free to supplement it with local groundwater. Such a change will require far-reaching legal and institutional reform, not only at the system level but also at the sub-basin and basin levels.

Legal Reform

Such a change will not only make the task of system management more manageable, but also provide the framework for enforceable entitlements of associations in different segments of a particular system. This approach can also be adopted in respect of non-agricultural uses through contracts with local pan-chayats. The allocation of entitlements for agricultural and non-agricultural uses for different segments of the command has to be decided through a process of con-sultation and negotiation of stakeholders at the system level. Issues of water quality, otherwise not included in the determination of entitlements, are also critical, and need to be internalized in this decision-making process at the system level.

Much the same approach can be used at the basin level also. However, the problem here is more com-plex because, in principle, all communities within its boundaries have a stake in where, how, and for what purposes the basin's resources are be used. To some extent, terrain, geology, and the spatial distribution of groundwater resources determine where storage is pos-sible. Moreover, how best to use available resources of the basin for the maximum benefit of the basin's popu-lation raises questions about how available resources can be used for the benefit of regions that do not have the advantage of storages, or groundwater for agricul-ture and basic domestic needs. For this reason, water-shed development—which will facilitate the more effective use of local rainfall for local use—should be viewed as a part of the water resources plan for the basin as a whole.

It is, therefore, important to evolve clear and consistent general principles by which the relative entitlements and rights of different segments and different user categories (including future users) in a river basin, and in the jurisdiction of a particular project, can be determined. At present, there are no clearly defined principles on which these matters are decided. The state claims the absolute right to decide them and change them at its discretion, without due process or public discussion. In the case of interstate rivers, these decisions—and resolving the conflicts over them—is left to tribunals. Their awards do not take into account all the considerations we have discussed. Nor are they equipped to deal with the complexities of the problem. The difficulty in getting objective information on relevant aspects, delays over decisions, the increasing tendency on the part of claimants to challenge them—or even refuse to abide by them—are worrisome trends. River basin authorities managed by representatives of all stakeholders and supported by expert advice on technical aspects of the problem based on reliable data but leaving the decisions to the basin authority is the best solution. But the states are unwilling to accept this. At the very least, such a system of collective decisions by representatives of stakeholders must be implemented at the level of individual systems and watershed development projects.

A clearer definition of 'rights' and 'entitlements' is a necessary but not a sufficient condition for their enforcement. Enforcement by state agencies even where rights are well defined is practically impossible and prohibitively expensive because of the huge number of individuals and plots to be monitored. It is also virtually impossible to design a tradable property regime with water as an economic commodity which can be allocated efficiently and equitably through the market mechanism.

It is essential to recognize that water is a common pool resource whose development and use must be subject to regulation in the public interest for the common good. While the state will have a significant role in the process, its developmental and promotional role must be kept distinct and separate from the regulatory function. Besides creating an environment which induces users to make prudent and efficient use of water, it is important to create an institutional structure with well-defined mechanisms of 'due process' to ensure that the observance of rights and obligations of users as well as suppliers, and changes therein, are regulated by an independent authority.

Also needed are more effective mechanisms for resolving disputes over the interpretation of rules and conflicts between uses and users, and between users and government agencies. It is essential to enunciate the basic principles on which disputes on entitlements ought to be resolved. The responsibility for making and enforcing rules consistent with these principles is a function of government and the institutions of water governance. Conscious effort must be made to encourage and facilitate the settlement of disputes and changes in entitlements through transparent negotiated compromises. Negotiated settlements between different systems, inter-basin and intra-basin, though imperfect and susceptible to political interference, may still be preferable to other methods of determining entitlements, since they have a larger degree of discipline and transparency.

When these mechanisms fail to resolve disputes, adjudication by courts will continue to be necessary. In the pre-Independence era, and right up to the 1970s, the judiciary looked primarily at the acts and facts that surrounded the disputes. From the 1980s onwards, it also began engaging in larger issues of equity, the economics of resource use, and the environment. There are considerable differences in judicial pronouncements on such basic issues concerning the interpretation of public good, prior appropriation rights versus optimum use, the balancing of competing interests, and the status of the 'eminent domain' doctrine as opposed to the 'public trust' doctrine. It points to the need for a systematic analysis of case law on water-related issues to assess the underlying principles of judgments, whether any systematic changes in this respect have been made over time, and to highlight the problems involved in ensuring that the judgments are, in fact, implemented. However, as seen above, adjudication cannot be effective unless there are agreed principles on which riparian rights are to be defined; the riparian states are willing to let disputes be mediated by independent judicial authority, and are committed to abide by their decisions.

Institutional Reform

These changes will, in turn, require far-reaching changes in legal and institutional arrangements. Currently, all functions involved in the development and efficient management of water resources—such as defining the nature and basis of entitlements, laying down broad principles and institutional mechanisms for deciding and implementing projects, regulating functions, and dispute settlement—are all conflated in the executive arm of the government. The state claims the exclusive right to decide where, how, and in what measure water is to be harnessed and utilized. Surface water development and management is entirely in the hands of government; groundwater exploitation is largely left to private initiative but with substantial support from the state and (purportedly) subject to state regulation. The responsibility—both in respect of sources and uses—is, however, vested with different agencies: minor irrigation is with one department; major and medium works with another; and groundwater with a third. Domestic and industrial water supply is handled by yet other departments/agencies.

Schemes are conceived, designed, appraised, constructed and managed by these departments. Often, these are done independently of each other, with little—or at best limited—consultation, not to mention coordination. Appraisals of the technical and

economic viability of projects are lax. Ad hoc arrangements for diverting water from irrigation projects
to non-agricultural uses are common. The common
pool character of water and the need for integrated
planning of sources and uses is conspicuously absent
in existing arrangements, even in respect of particular
areas or projects, and more so at the level of river basins
or sub-basins.

Experience has amply demonstrated that the present
system, whereby the government assumes the responsibility from conception through design, evaluation,
financing, and the construction of irrigation systems as
well as their continuing management wholly through
its bureaucracy, is incapable of achieving the above
objectives. The entire process at every stage is far too
opaque, open to interference and manipulation, and
without any effective incentive or mechanism to ensure
the economical use of resources in construction and
management, or to ensure that costs are fully recovered.
Besides introducing transparent criteria and procedures
to judge the soundness and viability of projects before
they go on stream, the management of systems must be
insulated from external interferences from politicians
and bureaucracy, and local power centres.

The beneficiaries of projects (new ones as well modernized old ones) must be required to contribute a share of the costs. This is necessary to give them a sense of stake and ownership. This can take the form of direct contributions in the form of labour, cash, or materials for the project as a whole; or entrusting the responsibility for constructing field channels and preparing lands below the outlet level for irrigation; or compensating oustees by giving them a part of their land. The sense of stake will be enhanced by ensuring that potential beneficiaries as well as those adversely affected are consulted in deciding the basic operational rules, governing the demarcation of areas to be benefited, and for compensation to project-affected people, allocations between different uses, permissible cropping patterns, and the scheduling of water under different contingencies. Continuing management should be entrusted to autonomous organizations with powers to make, change, and enforce rules, and levy and collect water rates on the condition that they become financially self-reliant.

Today, there is no transparency, due process, or accountability in the discharge of these functions. Instead of the larger and longer-term public interests,

the interests of the political executive and their parties and the bureaucracy dominate the whole process.
The governments' role should be limited to laying
down the broad legal and regulatory framework for
the development and management of water at the
system and basin levels, defining the rights and obligations of users vis-à-vis the system, and of individual
systems with higher-level bodies and the government;
as well as devising mechanisms and procedures for the
redressal of grievances and the settlement of disputes.
The mechanisms themselves must be independent of
the government, and vested with autonomous organizations operating at different levels of each river basin.

The internal structures of these organizations must
be such that user representatives participate in all levels
and functions of management. The involvement of
users in management provides them with space and
opportunities to evolve generally acceptable allocation
rules/criteria, monitor the actual performance of the
system, and to resolve conflicts through a process of
internal negotiation and compromise. It should also
provide a better mechanism for adapting rules in the
light of changing conditions. The intention behind the
suggestion for user associations at different tiers, and

the insistence on well-defined contracts between them and the system management in which their respective entitlements and obligations are defined, is to also create strong internal incentives for efficient and accountable management.

The concept of participatory irrigation management is now accepted, albeit hesitatingly and to a limited extent. Many states have enacted legislation to implement the concept. The focus, in practice, is on WUAs at the tertiary level, with a limited role in maintenance and collection of water charges. The power to make and change allocation rules and decide on water rates continues to vest with the government. Since there is no assurance of when and how much water will be available to a tertiary level, WUAs cannot be expected to make any significant difference to improving water-use efficiency.

Some states (notably Andhra Pradesh, Maharashtra, Odisha, and Haryana) have passed laws that go considerably further in having elected user representatives at all—including the top levels—of surface systems. Maharashtra has even created separate autonomous regulatory bodies to review decisions on allocations and pricing. In Andhra Pradesh, user associations have been made responsible for maintenance and repair works, and the collection of water rates. The government provides funds for maintenance from the budget, and allows user associations to retain a part of the collections. By all accounts, this has significantly improved the quality of works, and also reduced costs. But even in these states, the ministers and the bureaucracy are unwilling to hand over control of allocation rules, schedules, and pricing. Centralized political control over these matters remains.

Incentives for Conservation

Better laws and better institutions of governance are necessary but not sufficient conditions for turning the water sector around. Given that uses and users are numerous (running literally into millions), diffused, and connected in a complex network of interdependence, even the most competent, honest, and professional management cannot effectively monitor observance and enforce compliance with the suggested reorganization of institutions. It is essential to complement it with strong economic incentives to induce all concerned to observe rules and regulations, and individual users to behave in a manner conducive to achieving the overall objectives.

At present, the incentive system has perverse effects on water management. The government has taken the entire responsibility for funding, implementing, and managing surface irrigation. Users are not required to contribute any part of the cost. The pretence of collecting betterment levies has long since been given up. Users have no role in making or supervising allocation and scheduling decisions. Consequently, they feel no sense of stake or responsibility in the working of the system, and seek to shift all the blame for poor performance to the government. This is compounded by the government's water pricing policy. Providing water from public systems, and the energy used for pumping underground water at rates far below cost, leads to a larger and faster growth of demand for water, and greatly reduces the incentives for careful and prudent use.

Increasing water charges and the price of energy used for pumping, strong user involvement in management, insistence on the financially self-reliant operation of systems, and the strict enforcement of penalties for violations are necessary to create strong inducements for users to avoid wasteful use, and adopt water-saving practices. An equally important effect would be to dampen the growth of demand for freshwater. But this has to be done in such a way that user charges are related to the provision of a specified level of service quality at reasonable cost—both to be decided by an independent regulatory authority. It is necessary to reiterate that institutional reform and pricing/cost-sharing policies have to go in tandem in order to achieve a significant impact.

Increasing the effective cost of water for individual users, and aligning the relative costs for different uses to serve social priorities is essential. Revising water rates has become a political hot potato and (along with electricity) a major focus of competitive populism. Raising water rates is seen as an invitation to electoral disaster, and few governments, irrespective of party affiliation, are willing to take the risk. It is clearly difficult to get politicians to even consider, let alone implement, a steep revision in one go. A graduated approach is, thus, essential. A good first step would be to rationalize the existing area rates on the basis of the relative irrigation requirements by season and crop in different regions. It would approximate to a volumetric charge without actually having to measure volumes delivered to individual users. This could be followed by the strategy adopted by Maharashtra where a progressive increase in rates over a five-year period is announced in advance. This way, users can be given clear advance signals of the government's long-term aims regarding the level of cost recovery as well as reasonable time for them to adjust their use patterns accordingly.

The aim should be to give a clear indication that full cost recovery is to be achieved over a period of time. For this purpose, governments should adopt a policy of automatic indexing of water rates to operation and maintenance costs, or product prices. Had such a policy been followed from the 1970s, the increase required to meet capital charges would have been far more manageable. Thus, the wholesale price index in 1993–4 was nearly four times the level in 1977–8. Assuming no change in collection efficiency, indexing water rates to, say, the wholesale price index would have raised revenues to Rs 21 billion by 1993–4, compared to the actual realization of Rs 4.5 billion. The required realization for full cost recovery would have been only two-and-a-half times the collection on the basis of the indexed rate, which is far less formidable compared to

the tenfold rise needed on the basis of current realizations. Graduated additions over the indexed rate could
then be made in such a way that capital charges could
also be recovered fully over a specified period of, say,
10 years.

The credibility of government's intention about its
goals, and its seriousness about fairness to users will be
enhanced if a mechanism is created for an independent review of reported investments in all projects to
allow for over-capitalization due to poor design and
inefficient implementation and arrive at a fair basis for
determining the capital charges component of water
rates. Such an approach has, however, to contend with
the argument that an increase in rates should not be
disproportionately large in relation to the increase in
productivity due to irrigation, and that steep increases
will not be justified unless the quality of irrigation
service improves significantly. In this connection, it is
worth noting that, on average, during the early 1980s
full cost recovery, which called for a tenfold rise in
revenue, meant that farmers would have had to pay
nearly 30 per cent of the incremental productivity of
irrigated land as water charge. This would naturally
be considered unreasonably high. However, one must

also bear in mind the following factors which reduce effective incidence even at current low rates: (a) the above estimates of the differential between irrigated and rainfed productivity is understated; (b) there is considerable under-recording of total area irrigated by major and medium works, especially of area under crops carrying higher rates; and (c) the assessed dues are not fully collected. They underscore the importance of the scrupulously strict assessment of crop-wise areas irrigated, and ensuring that dues are collected fully and promptly. In both respects, the quality of governance of irrigation systems leaves much to be desired.

The extent of rate increases will obviously depend on the incidence of under-assessment and leakages. The extent of the latter is not known; they are also likely to vary a great deal between regions. It is, there-fore, essential to commission a systematic and objective assessment for each system of the area actually receiv-ing irrigation, the area under various crops, and their productivity. Even after these adjustments, there is no doubt that full cost recovery will mean a substantial increase in the incidence of water charges relative to output at current levels of water-use efficiency and productivity.

Small-scale Local Irrigation Works and Watershed Development

The importance of tanks and ponds lies not in the extent of water they supply or the area they irrigate, but the fact that they are the main source of water for domestic and agricultural use in a very large majority of villages. A large proportion of them are managed by local bodies and communities based on time-honoured conventions. In some cases—usually larger multi-village tanks—governments have a more direct presence in water regulation. As with large surface systems, governments have assumed the authority and responsibility for repairing major damages, and for the modernization of existing facilities and (on a limited scale) for construction of new works. The government plays little role in privately owned works which are numerous, and though small, these are vital in storing rainwater and facilitating groundwater recharge in numerous communities.

Programmes for rehabilitation and modernization are included in public sector plans. Some states have spent substantial amounts of money on these. The selection of tanks, the kinds of works taken up, and

181

the modalities of implementation have been decided entirely by government departments without any consultation or involvement of communities. Most of the work has been entrusted to contractors, without any mechanisms for supervision and the audit of works done. They do not seem to have made any significant increase in water availability or irrigated area. Further large increases that are now being proposed will be just as unfruitful unless communities are left to decide what improvements are needed, and how the works are to be implemented under the supervision of the panchayats.

There is need to decentralize responsibility and authority in this sphere to panchayati raj institutions which can use public funds available through numerous rural development and employment programmes. There is a tradition of beneficiary communities participating or contributing to the proper maintenance and management of tanks. The collective interest of users whose livelihood is dependent on water is the rationale for this practice which is not too robust currently, but has not died out, and may yet be revitalized in many cases. The present trend of ignoring existing (often functional) informal local institutions, and the insistence on the formation of WUAs as preconditions for the government undertaking modernization programmes, is quite the wrong thing to do. Informal local institutions need to be revived, and an environment conducive to their being strengthened is necessary. The decentralization of responsibility to panchayats, giving them the legal basis for working out community-level arrangements and mechanisms appropriate to local conditions, can help strengthen them. The government's role should be limited to providing technical support and commissioning independent evaluations.

Much the same is true of watershed development programmes which have become the main instrument for soil and water conservation in rainfed lands. The idea is to retain as much of the local rainfall for local use by reducing surface runoff, and trapping reduction to increase soil moisture, storage in local ponds, and facilitate greater recharge of local aquifers. Being limited by the extent of local rainfall, the potential increase in water availability is bound to be quite small compared to irrigation works. But they could make a substantial difference to water for local use over rainfed areas which, after all, comprise the major part of land in the country. The scale and scope of this programme has greatly expanded into a national programme for integrated watershed development. Its aim is not only to increase local water availability, but to use it in a planned manner to increase the biomass in common lands and the productivity of agricultural land.

Interventions have to be planned in the light of conditions and possibilities specific to each location. These vary greatly across regions, and also across micro watersheds within a village or group of contiguous villages. Moreover, these interventions have to be done for the watershed as a whole, and for individual pieces of land. An enforceable consensus on the sharing of costs and benefits has to be based on collective decisions on how the additional water is to be allocated between private and common lands, and between different private owners for increasing overall biomass production and its sharing between different sections. This is an entirely new undertaking, which calls for creating a framework for setting and nurturing appropriate institutions for collective planning and management. That it is difficult is obvious. But that it is not insuperable is also evident from many, though as yet scattered and limited, successful experiences of NGO initiatives.

These aspects have been emphasized by official committees charged with suggesting appropriate institutional arrangements for the programme. However, the suggestions have been given the go-by, with the government choosing to create a national rainfed area development authority for allocating and transferring funds to panchayats and districts through state governments on the basis of overall guidelines regarding the scope and content of the works to be undertaken, the mechanisms for implementation at the ground level, and for monitoring it. That the guidelines leave little room for adaptation to local conditions is a major problem. So is the fact that the central monitoring of implementation of such a huge and dispersed programme is impossible. Moreover, the concept of local communities planning and implementing the programme finds little favour with state governments and the political class. Local watershed committees that have been set up are non-functional. The task of deciding and implementing needed physical works is left to the functionaries of line departments. They work in isolation and not in collaboration, and without any consultation with the community. The programme is in dire need of a drastic overhaul.

The following measures assume urgency:

- Transferring funds allocated to the programme to various operating levels down to the panchayat level on the basis of well-defined criteria
- Making participation in the national programme optional but strictly conditional on the acceptance and giving resources to and vesting authority in elected panchayats at the ground level
- Trying out different approaches—entirely under state governments, the Rural Infrastructure Development Fund (RIDF) model of National Bank for Agriculture and Rural Development, and initiatives of local NGOs—so that their relative performance can be better understood and appreciated
- Collating and disseminating knowledge and experience of techniques relevant to watershed development under different agro-climatic and terrain conditions in different countries and in different regions of the country
- Preparing, maintaining, and updating a list of NGOs with experience and a proven record
- Official mobilization for collective functioning before, during, and after the project

Implementation at the panchayat level should:

- develop formats for maintenance of basic records of expenditures incurred and work done and for reporting the information to the community, upper-tier organizations, and to the rainfed authority;
- liaise with the research system to focus on generating technologies and practices for sustained increases in productivity of rainfed areas, and address problems encountered by communities under different agro-climatic conditions;
- maintain a roster of experts who are available for providing technical, financial control, and managerial advice to the operating agencies on different aspects;
- create a system for reviewing the implementation of projects at different levels through sample surveys done through independent research organizations;
- develop a network of independent research institutions to assess, in selected watersheds, the conditions of water availability, land use, stock, and flow of crop and non-crop biomass, regulation of land and water use, access to usufruct of common lands, and the general state of the economy before, during, and

periodically for many years after the completion of the project; and

- explore actively the use of remote sensing, combined with appropriate ground truth verification, for getting reliable information on the state of land use, vegetation, moisture conditions, location, and conditions of conservation structures and biomass.

The focus must shift to these tasks if the new initiative is to have reasonable chance of success. And it is vital that the proposed authority should not have any executive functions but limit itself to facilitation, advice, and independent monitoring of implementation and impact evaluation.

9

Prospects for Reform

The current ways in which water resource development is planned, implemented, and managed is unsatisfactory and untenable. Currently, the state and its
executive agencies have assumed, and exercise, almost
unfettered authority for legislating the overall legal
framework, for deciding concrete policies, programmes,
and measures for all these functions as well as running
their management at all levels. Experience has shown
serious weaknesses in this arrangement.

Under the Constitution, governments of the states
constituting the Union are free to decide and implement programmes for the development of water
within their territorial domains except in respect
of interstate rivers. The Centre's formal authority
is limited to deciding entitlements of riparian states,

resolving interstate disputes over water, and giving its prior approval for new projects on these rivers. Central governments of all political hues (even those which had a comfortable parliamentary majority) have been neither willing, nor able, to exercise even this limited authority. Efforts through political consultative mechanisms for forging a national consensus on important issues have resulted only in bald declarations, leaving room for all governments to do as they please.

The responsibility for the planning and implementation of programmes for different purposes and from different sources is highly fragmented, both at the Centre and in the states. Governments at all levels are obsessed with projects for augmenting water supplies to satisfy the growing demand for domestic uses, agriculture, and industry to the neglect of the downside effects on the environment, efficiency, and sustainable use. The conflation of developmental, managerial, and regulatory functions within the government has given the governing elite enormous scope and opportunity to manipulate the use of public resources to serve the political interests of ruling parties. They have been able exercise this authority with impunity by deliberately (i) neglecting to create effective mechanisms to redress grievances, (ii) restricting the availability of data open to public scrutiny and independent research, and (iii) preventing a meaningful discussion of issues by politicizing public discourse on water.

All these have contributed to the chaotic state of water resource programmes, reflected in spiralling costs and delays in completion of projects, rampant rule violations, pervasive corruption, and near-anarchy in the management of systems. Under these conditions, integrated planning and the management of water for different uses from different interrelated sources are hardly possible without far-reaching changes in strategy, policies, and institutional arrangements.

Being a common pool resource, the development and use of water must be regulated in the public interest. This includes not merely meeting the varied needs for improving people's living conditions but also be consistent with equitable access, long-term sustainability, and environmental health. The state and the institutions of governance must necessarily play a key role for this purpose. However, the government's role should be limited to determining the broad objectives of water resource development. It should lay down the general principles and processes by which competing claims of different uses can remain balanced. It should specify the institutional locus for deciding these matters at various levels. It should also decide the sources and modes of financing and cost recovery, as well as provide the legal framework within which entities remain responsible both for the construction and management of systems and for regulatory and conflict-resolution activities remaining functional. Given that the state is committed to investing large amounts of public funds in water resource development, it is essential that the internal evaluation of project proposals be made transparent, professional, and available for public scrutiny. Governments must be divested of regulatory, conflict resolution, and evaluation functions. These must be entrusted to independent professional bodies and research organizations.

Ideally, the natural hydrological regions delineated by river basins, with tiers covering their constituent sub-basins, micro watersheds, and projects are the most appropriate units for the integrated planning and management of different sources of water. The basis and criteria for the allocation of water between different segments of a basin/sub-basin at different levels should be defined by the state. But the authority and responsibility for performing these functions must be taken out of government departments. They should be vested with institutions autonomous of the government, and manned by independent professionals with expertise and experience.

For the continuing management of systems, it is essential to set up stakeholder-managed organizations at the basin, project, and watershed management levels. These should be (a) autonomous of government; (b) be managed by elected representatives of user groups/ users, with the freedom to make and enforce rules/ contracts, as well as levy and collect fees for water supplied; (c) responsible for maintenance and repairs; and (d) empowered to make and change rules, and devise enforcement strategies consistent with the requirements not only of the fair distribution of benefits but also of sustainable use. Ideally, they should be required to meet, in due course, the cost of water obtained from the higher-tier sources, operation and maintenance expenditures, and capital charges from user fees without government subventions. In order to motivate user communities to take these responsibilities seriously, it is important that beneficiaries of individual systems be required to contribute a substantial part of capital investments in new projects as well as for the improvement of existing ones.

Such internal reorganization of water management would increase the availability of information about the requirements for various uses specific to a region/system. It would enable more flexible management of water capable of being adapted to diverse and changing local needs. It would also facilitate the effective monitoring and enforcement of rule compliance as well as a quicker resolution of internal conflicts through informal negotiations and compromise. In order to avail themselves of these advantages, it is essential that different claimants to the water available across different regions and systems within a basin, as well as within each system have clearly defined entitlements.

A clear and explicit enunciation of the nature and scope of 'water rights' is essential. That they can only be 'user rights' is obvious. The scope of the 'rights' must not be restricted to the requirements for human use. They must also provide adequately for the protection of the environment, and for long-term sustainability. Fixed and permanent entitlements are not desirable because they make adaptation to changes in the technology of extraction and use—and in level and patterns of demand—very difficult. There is much to be said for moving towards a system in which the entitlements of regions/systems—decided by negotiation or by judicial/quasi-judicial mechanisms—are formalized into contracts between entities that control supplies, on the one hand, and the different systems that depend on these supplies, on the other.

These contracts should specify both the rights of the different systems to get their entitlements, and the obligations of the upper tiers of the basin organization to ensure that they are delivered. They must also specify penalties for the violation of terms on either side, which must be enforceable through courts if the need arises. In order to facilitate the orderly adaptation to changing conditions of supply and demand, it is desirable to make contractual rights tenable for reasonably long yet specified periods of time which can be subject to renegotiation at the end of the period. These processes should be based on negotiated compromises between different stakeholders through their elected managements.

Credible internal mechanisms for the articulation of grievances and disputes, and their expeditious resolution—with provision for appeal to adjudication by outside institutions—are essential. At the same time, a great deal needs to be done to facilitate better, quicker, and fairer handling of these matters within water management organizations at various levels. Extrajudicial mechanisms—especially arbitration and negotiation—need to be given more scope, and be actively encouraged.

Civil society and non-governmental researchers can buttress these efforts in significant ways. Experience has demonstrated that concerted pressures exerted by them can induce changes in programmes and policies. They are playing an increasingly important role in highlighting deficiencies and grievances, and in exerting pressure for corrective action. Many of the recent reform initiatives have responded to civil society critiques. Non-governmental organizations—independently and in cooperation with official agencies—are exploring and experimenting with better ways to manage water more efficiently and equitably. Their active engagement in the public discourse on water-related matters has also led to more information being available in the public domain, and has influenced some significant changes in larger water-related policies. The widening and deepening of this engagement needs to be encouraged and fostered.

The various components of reform must be viewed as a totality comprising a coherent and mutually reinforcing set of measures which address interrelated problems in different aspects of water resource management. Concerted and carefully phased action on all components (technical, institutional, and economic) is essential for the significant improvement in water resource management at a systemic level. Selective and piecemeal changes on particular aspects will not be effective. For instance, institutional reforms may help improve some aspects of water-use efficiency, but they may not necessarily bring about improvement in the equitable and sustainable use of water. Improvements in both the design as well as regulatory devices in distribution systems can reduce avoidable wastes while conveying water to the fields within an irrigation command. However, the extent to which this can be done is constrained by technical factors, and costs. Moreover, the inherent difficulties in coordinating the timing and distribution of supplies from different sources (to maintain optimum moisture regimes for all crops) have not yet been solved. The instruments being used to address this problem—for example, imposing restrictions on cropping patterns—have proved ineffective.

The widespread tendency to overuse irrigation water is partly due to uncertainties in timing and in the quantum of supplies. A far more important cause is the government's policy of charging highly subsidized rates for canal water and energy (for pumping). This is compounded by the laxity in the collection of dues. Because of this, users have little incentive to conserve water. Moreover, with available yield-augmenting technology biased in favour of irrigated crops, the differential between returns on irrigated crops—as opposed to rainfed agriculture—have widened. This has induced a faster growth in the demand for irrigation. With demand for non-agricultural uses also growing rapidly, the overall demand for water is far in excess of available supplies; and the gap is growing.

Under these circumstances, it is hardly surprising that violations of rules and regulations on water use are rampant, and that conflicts between uses and users at all levels are becoming increasingly widespread and unmanageable. This hiatus cannot be addressed by the physical improvement of systems or by the restructuring of institutions only. The way out seems to lie in creating environments in which users have strong incentives to conserve water, and use it more prudently. It is for this reason that a substantial increase in user charges—to levels more commensurate with costs—must be an essential and crucial element of reform. This must be combined with a shift from the current system of distribution of water to individual plots and cropping pattern restrictions to one of bulk supply of specified volumes of water—and their timing and duration—to user associations at the ground level.

Achieving equity and sustainability is difficult. This will remain so unless the pressure of overall excess demand—characteristic of both surface and groundwater systems—over large parts of the country, is reduced. Even with restructured institutions, not all stakeholder interests are effectively represented in elected boards. This is especially true of the poor and the under-privileged, and of those concerned with the long-term environmental aspects of resource use. Configurations of power within these organizations, and their links to the wider political sphere, though non-formal, will continue to play an important role. In so far as improved management and higher user charges induce some conservation in existing systems, the resulting increase in supply effectively available for use will also help users—especially those with relatively weak capability and voice—in deciding utilization.

Sustainability has to be addressed at a systemic level. Here the task is even more difficult because renewable and potentially utilizable supplies are strictly finite, and current levels of utilization are close to, and in some cases exceed, this limit. Starting on many new projects or expanding groundwater use in the interest of reducing regional disparities are dangerous options in the long term, and need careful watching. If anything, they will aggravate the adverse effects of overexploitation, displacement, and ecological damage. Such programmes can only be handled by the imposition of stricter standards in assessing their environmental consequences, and in their tough enforcement. However, the prospects of this actually being done remain bleak.

Given that the potential for using renewable supplies of surface and groundwater to supplement rainfall is already reaching the limit, it is important to increase local water supply. This can be done by making more effective use of local rainfall for agricultural and domestic use in rainfed areas, and in the degraded upper catchments of streams and rivers. Over wide areas, soil erosion (and the consequent degradation of land) has reduced the capacity of the soil to absorb and retain water from natural rainfall so that small local surface storages and groundwater aquifers can be fed. These trends can be substantially mitigated through rainwater harvesting, erosion control, and increasing the forest and vegetative cover of the upper catchments through integrated watershed development. Slowing down the pace of surface runoff from rainfall, and extending its duration by using traditional wisdom and modern techniques, can substantially increase the proportion of water from local rainfall available for domestic use, and for increasing useful biomass output. This is indeed the basic concept underlying the national integrated water-shed programme.

While substantial outlays are being made for this programme, it suffers from serious deficiencies in design and implementation as well as in its institutional arrangements which are similar to those which affect water resource development. In essential features, the corrective action needed—ensuring integrated planning, decentralization of responsibility to stakeholder-managed institutions, community regulation of land, increased water supply, and equitable distribution of access and use—are much the same as outlined earlier. Properly managed, these programmes can, in varying degrees across regions, help increase overall productivity of rainfed lands. Though their impact on water availability and agricultural productivity will be variable—and no doubt they will not bring rainfed lands on a par with irrigated tracts—they will make a substantial contribution to raising incomes and the living conditions in rainfed areas.

Current Reform Initiatives

Deficiencies in existing institutional and policy regimes, and the need for reforms to address them, have been articulated by many official committees, evaluation studies, academic researchers, and NGOs. This has led to a number of initiatives for the speedier utilization of potential through command area development programmes. These include better regulation of water distribution in surface irrigation, facilitating the conjunctive use of surface and canal water, setting up WUAs for greater user participation in water management, and exploring ways to control pollution.

These have been pursued fitfully and hesitantly. Their scale and scope has been far too limited: for instance, they do not cover small surface works and groundwater, or uses other than irrigation. Governments have been unwilling to even consider raising water charges. On the contrary, their policies have moved in the retrograde direction of lowering them.

In response to sustained pressure from nongovernmental organizations and activists—and reinforced by prodding from international lending agencies—some state governments (notably Andhra Pradesh, Maharashtra, and Odisha) have recently made efforts to attempt a basic restructuring of the system. These are welcome developments. They are aimed at giving elected user representatives a larger and more effective role in managing systems at all levels, and establishing independent regulatory agencies. These have the authority to (i) review the basis for the state's overall policy for water allocation, (ii) assess water-pricing policies, (iii) evaluate operations at the systems level, and change them if necessary; and (iv) enable/induce WUAs to take greater responsibility for the maintenance of distribution networks, regulation of water supply, and the collection of user charges. These reforms are still evolving. Experience has brought out many important gaps in design, and difficulties in implementation.

Even at the level of WUAs, the coverage, scope, and effectiveness of their activities are uneven. For instance, the reform initiative of Andhra Pradesh focuses primarily on expanding the coverage of WUAs with elected managements, and entrusting them with the responsibility only for maintenance. The programme is reported to be doing well, and has resulted in significant improvement in the distribution network, and the conditions of water supply at the tertiary level. However, most other aspects of the management of intra-basin and inter-system water allocation rules and schedules remain with the government.

The structure envisaged by the Maharashtra reformers is far more comprehensive. It envisages entrusting the WUAs with the maintenance and collection of water charges as well as the allocation of water between uses and users within their command. The volume of water they get is based on a formal contract awarded to them, under a formal MoU with the system. There is also a provision for a federation of WUAs and their representation in the system management.

System-level management can decide the entitlements of different WUAs to canal water and determine user rates with the approval of an independent regulatory authority. However, they have no say over use of groundwater. The power to decide intra-basin allocations and groundwater regulations remains with the state government. The coverage of this arrangement is increasing, but is still limited.

Impediments

Fragmented Perspectives

Evidently, governments and their water resource agencies still do not appreciate these complexities. They continue to think and act in isolation. The situation is much worse in other states. Everywhere, there is enormous resistance to structural reforms that will loosen the control of executive agencies, and the influence of the political class over water resource management. Government agencies are responsible for planning, supply, and distribution for different uses, and actual users are more concerned with increasing supply. Efficiency and sustainability are left to other agencies. There is no mechanism in the decision-making or implementation process for meaningful interaction between planners, water supply managers, users, and environmental experts.

The central government is no exception. The National Water Policy statement, formulated in consultation with and approved by the states, has called for 'integrated water management' for 'efficient, equitable and sustainable use of water'. However, neither the Ministry of Water Resources nor the Planning Commission has taken any initiative to articulate the operational implications of this declaration, or to persuade its own agencies and the states to change their approach to planning strategies.

Lack of Data and Analysis

It is a regrettable fact that public policies and plans for the water sector—and indeed a great deal of public debate—are based on inadequate information and analysis. Available data are, for the most part estimates, based on patchy, incomplete information, and assumptions whose validity has not been rigorously validated. The scope and quality of data based on the actual measurements of various elements needed to assess the potential and utilization for various purposes, even at an aggregate level, is very limited. Disaggregated data for regions and individual systems is even more so. Moreover, very little of the results of these efforts is in the public domain. Much of the data is treated as classified. Progress in recent initiatives to improve the coverage and techniques of measurement of key hydrological data at the basin and sub-basin levels has fallen short of expectations. Also, the digitization of all available water-related data in an integrated framework, and their availability on the web in any meaningful way has yet to happen.

One would have thought that while dealing with technically complex and socially sensitive issues relating to water, governments and lending agencies would collect reliable information and use professionally competent analyses for taking decisions. These analyses could include examining alternative courses of action, keeping track of actual implementation and its impact, and learning from an analysis of differences between realized processes and outcomes, relative to expectations. On the contrary, government agencies vested with these functions are noticeably reluctant to collect reliable information, and use it for professionally competent analysis in decision-making. International funding agencies like the World Bank and the ADB that offer 'expert' advice on water-related matters with such confidence—and have lent large amounts for water resource projects—invest next to nothing in improving the knowledge base for the lending decisions, or even an objective assessment of the performance of the projects they finance.

Paucity of information in the public domain imposes a severe constraint on the contribution that independent professional research can make to clarify issues, and provide possible solutions along with their implications. Decision-making within the government at all levels suffers from a huge knowledge deficit, and lack of rigorous, data-based analyses. Such analyses that are made—or commissioned—are not open to public scrutiny. Independent research is hampered by difficulties in accessing information collected by public agencies, and their meagre interest in supporting it. Under these conditions, informed public discussion—be it in the councils of government, legislatures, or among the public—of programmes and policies, the basis and merits of positions taken by different interests groups, and the achievement of a reasonable workable compromise is vitiated.

Many measures are necessary to address these lacunae.

- The National Hydrology project as well as the existing integrated water resources information system should be expanded to cover more details, and incorporate more disaggregated data. All water-related information must be made accessible under the Freedom of Information law.

- The central government should take the initiative to lay down a uniform framework of concepts, content, and the reporting of information on the status of reservoirs, the location and extent of area irrigated, and the behaviour of groundwater tables, and changes therein.

- Since states are reluctant to part with information, and tend to use information selectively, there is a strong case for the Centre to collect and disseminate these basic data directly, using a combination of remote-sensing and sample surveys. The responsibility for this should be entrusted to a special agency autonomous of executive departments, and include non-governmental professionals.

- The Centre should actively encourage and support non-governmental researchers and organizations to undertake in-depth studies, and provide independent analyses. It should also fund a long-term institutionalized programme of research to track changes in the physical condition, maintenance and operation, water availability and efficiency of its use, in cropping patterns and productivity, and in the environment in selected surface systems as well as groundwater in select areas.

- This calls for substantially larger allocations for research by scholars and institutions outside government, as well as a thorough review of the work done by governmental research institutions (which currently absorb the bulk of allocations for research), and suggest ways to promote greater interaction and collaboration with universities and non-governmental institutions.

Difficulties in Implementation

Extending and improving reform initiatives is, of course, essential. In doing so, taking cognizance of constraints experienced by ground-level autonomous organizations in states that are trying to implement structural reforms is necessary. Greater authority over water allocation and management needs to be vested with autonomous organizations for both surface and groundwater at the basin and sub-basin levels. But, to exercise this authority, they need to know how much water is being used for what purpose, within and outside the command of existing users. Validated data even for public systems is scanty. That unauthorized use outside the command is widespread makes the problem of deciding entitlements even more difficult. In the preparatory phase of reform, it is, therefore, essential to systematically collect these data with the active involvement of local panchayats/WUAs, guided by local NGOs. These data, combined with an objective assessment of requirements, could be the basis on which the relative claims of the authorized and unauthorized uses/users could be treated in redefining entitlements under the new regime.

In Maharashtra, the transfer of responsibility for maintenance and water allocation to WUAs is conditional on the government undertaking major repairs to restore the physical condition of the distributaries feeding the outlets. Failure to fulfil this commitment is reported to be impeding the process.

The role of local WUAs is limited to maintenance, and the repair of distributaries and field channels in their command and, in some cases, helping to improve the collection of water fees. When, with what frequency, and how much water they will get at their outlets, is left to be decided by the management at the system and by higher levels. Since representatives of WUAs hardly play any role in these matters, their ability to improve the efficiency of water use is severely limited. This constraint can be eased by ensuring reasonable assurance of the duration and quantum of water to outlet associations. Giving them the authority to regulate groundwater use in their command is very essential. These are to be decided through a consensus among the users within the command. Evolving flexible arrangements for this purpose, suited to specific local conditions, is a challenge for the associations. That they are unused to this mode of functioning makes for difficulties which can be overcome only through an evolutionary process of trial and error, and learning from experience.

Political Resistance to Reform

These tasks are the more daunting because of the apathy and skepticism (bordering on hostility) of stakeholders to any significant change in the status quo, and the opposition of a large and influential segment of the rural electorate which has got used to permissive water governance, violation of rules with impunity, and a regime of highly subsidized water and electricity rates. They clamour for more and cheaper water, unmindful of the true dimensions and seriousness of the crisis caused by the profligate and inefficient use of water, encouraged and abetted by the present regime. The difficulties are compounded by the entrenched opposition from the political class cutting across party lines, and the water bureaucracies who have enormous power under the current system, and have utilized it in various ways to serve their own interests. Politicians who realize the long-term consequences of allowing the present situation to continue and recognize the need for reform are rare. Even they are constrained to attach greater weight to short-term electoral compulsions.

Overcoming Impediments

Daunting as these impediments are, water is far too important a natural resource to let the drift continue. Proactive effort is necessary to educate the political class and the main stakeholder interests about the seriousness of the consequences. Before persuading them about the rationale for the broad approach to reform and its potential benefits, it is necessary to create an atmosphere more conducive to reform. Concrete historical and contemporary examples of the dire social, economic, and ecological consequences of overexploitation and misuse of water as well as the beneficial effects obtained by the key elements of reforms—both individually and collectively—need to be marshalled and highlighted. Professionals, both inside and outside government and civil society organizations, have the responsibility to play a leading role in mounting an organized campaign for this purpose.

There are signs—as yet limited and diffused—of farmers taking an active interest in improving the quality of irrigation, especially when faced with significant reductions in available supplies. The creation of WUAs and the governments' declared commitment to 'turning over' the management to users seem to have kindled both awareness and interest in these matters among the farming community.

Political parties, for the most part, still shun any attempt at raising water rates, considering this suicidal. However, we can expect—or at least hope—that the parlous state of public finances, and the fact that subsidized supplies lead to a wasteful use of water as well as cuts into resources for socio-economic infrastructure, will induce at least a few of them to address the issue. This inclination can be strengthened through concrete examples of water-saving and increased productivity being achieved through an assured but regulated volume of water supply to the individual user even as its cost is raised.

It is also important to highlight the need to give WUAs a larger role in all facets of water management, and address problems in implementing reforms at the ground level. This would mean (a) reducing the role of the government to laying down broad policy and legal frameworks; (b) establishing autonomous basin organizations and regulatory authorities; (c) giving them a wider role in actual management, with a clearer demarcation of their spheres of authority and responsibility; and (d) making periodic independent evaluations of performance and impact on the water situation mandatory.

A better understanding of the problems in carrying out various elements of reforms, and a convincing demonstration of its impact in terms of water saving and increased productivity, would become immediately possible by implementing all elements of the reform package at the system level. The selection of these projects as well as their implementation, monitoring their progress, and ensuring a rigorous assessment of their impact over a reasonably long period of time should be entrusted to a special expert group consisting of water managers from the central and state governments, and non-official experts, with the Centre meeting the full cost.

The campaign for reform of leadership positions requires the mobilization of non-official experts and NGOs knowledgeable about water sector management. It is the National Planning Commission which must help effect this mobilization, and also provide a much-needed breadth of perspective.

Further Reading

Introduction

Wikepedia provides a fairly extensive review of the historical evolution of water control systems in different parts of the world. Needham, Joseph A. (1971), *Science and Civilisation in China*, volume IV. Cambridge: Cambridge University Press describes, in considerable and fascinating detail, the techniques of food control and irrigation in ancient and medieval China, and also of techniques used for the construction of tanks in Sri Lanka and South India.

For an overview of the evolution and current status of the world's water resource potential and use, including the conceptual framework and empirical estimates, see Shiklomonov, Igor A. and Jeanna A. Balonishnikova (2003), *World Water Use and Water Availability: Trends, Scenarios, Consequences* (accessible on http://iashs.info/redbooks/a281/iahs_281_358.pdf, last accessed in August 2012).

Data cited in this section are taken from Shiklomonov, Igor A. (1999), 'World Water Resources at the Turn of the Century', monograph prepared for the International Hydrology Project of UNESCO, available at the Pacific Institute website on 'The World's Water', http://www.worldwater.org/ last accessed in August 2012.

For an overview of the growth of groundwater extraction and use, see Shah, Tushaar (2006), 'Groundwater and Human Development: Challenges and Opportunities in Livelihoods and Environment', in B.R. Sharma, K. Villholth, and K.D. Sharma (eds), Groundwater Research and Management: Integrating Science into Management Decisions. Proceedings of IWMI-ITP-NH International Workshop on 'Creating Synergy between Groundwater Research and Management in South and Southeast Asia', IWMI, Colombo, pp. 14–26, Groundwater Governance in Asia Series-1.

Chapter 1

Estimates of water potential and utilization are mostly taken from publications of the Central Water Commission, Central Groundwater Board, and the Indian Meteorological Department.

A recent (2011) report on 'Data Water Database Development and Management', prepared by the Working Group of the Planning Commission, provides a detailed critical review of the coverage, methodology, and limitations of the estimates, and makes many suggestions for improvement of the database.

For a discussion of the role of climate in determining the need for, possibilities of, and the nature of irrigation, and the way it is managed, and comparisons between different parts of Asia, see Vaidyanathan, A. (1999), *Water Resources Management: Institutions and Irrigation Development in India*. New Delhi: Oxford University Press. The book also contains a select, though dated, bibliography of the literature. References to more recent international work are accessible on the IWMI website.

Data cited in Table 5 are taken from the website of the Tyndall Centre for Climatic Research, available at http://www.cru.uea.ac.uk, last accessed in August 2012. Those cited in Table 6 is taken from Government of India [GoI], *Water and Related Statistics 2007*. New Delhi: Central Water Commission.

Chapter 2

Besides the reports of various Famine Enquiry committees and the Irrigation Commission of 1903, the Indian National Committee on Irrigation development has published histories of the development of irrigation, drainage, and flood control in India, and also in some states.

Data for recent decades on developments in surface and groundwater irrigation, overall and region-wise, are accessible at http://www.fao.org/nr/water/aquastat/main/index.stm, last accessed in August 2012.

Data cited in Table 7 is taken from Government of India (2005), *Report of the Third Census of Minor Irrigation 2000–1*. New Delhi: Ministry of Water Resources.

The discussion of minor surface irrigation works and their management draws on extensive field studies on tanks conducted by researchers at the Madras Institute of Development Studies, Chennai; Institute of Social and Economic Change, Bangalore; and the Centre for Development Studies, Thiruvananthapuram.

Chapter 3

Estimates of source-wise net irrigated area, total and crop-wise irrigated area cited in this chapter are based on data on land-use and crop-area statistics published by the Directorate of Economics and Statistics of the Ministry of Agriculture.

In the absence of any other estimate by official agencies, expert committees, or independent researchers, the overall value of output per hectare (and per unit of consumptive water use) for irrigated and unirrigated crops overall, and in different regions cited in this chapter are based on Vaidyanathan, A. and K. Sivasubramanian (2004), 'Efficiency of Water Use in Indian Agriculture', Working Paper No. 183, Madras Institute of Development Studies, Chennai.

Given data limitations, these estimates are necessarily approximate. Our focus and emphasis is on the striking patterns of variation across regions, and plausible explanations for them.

Vaidyanathan, A. (2006), *India's Water Resources: Contemporary Issues on Irrigation*. New Delhi: Oxford University Press.

Vaidyanathan, A. (2010), *Agricultural Growth in India: Role of Technology, Incentives, and Institutions*. New Delhi: Oxford University Press.

Chapter 4

Discussion in this chapter is based on a review of reports of several official committees, publications of the Planning Commission, non-government researchers, and critical evaluations of the performance of government programmes.

For a good overview, see Ramaswamy Iyer, R. [ed.] (2009), *Water and the Laws in India*. New Delhi: Sage Publications.

Chapter 5

For a more detailed account of the evolution of pricing policy for irrigation water and its actual implementation, see Government of India (1992), *Report of the Committee on Pricing of Irrigation Water for a Comprehensive Programme of Legal, Institutional, and Economic Reforms for Better Management of Water*. New Delhi: Planning Commission.

Data on the financial performance of public sector irrigation projects of different types are available in Government
of India (GoI), *Water and Related Statistics 2008*. New Delhi:
Central Water Commission.

'Unrecovered' costs of public irrigation systems and of
electricity supplied to agriculture for private well irrigation
gives a measure of the implicit subsides on these inputs. It
includes the difference between actual current expenditures
on the operation and maintenance of facilities as well as the
interest and depreciation on cumulative capital investments
at current prices. The basis, rationale, and procedures for
estimation are spelt out in Srivatsava, D.K., C. Bhujanga
Rao, Pinaki Chakravarthy, and T.S. Rangamannar (2003),
*Budgetary Subsidies in India: Subsidizing Social and Economic
Services*. New Delhi: National Institute of Public Finance
and Policy. Estimates presented in this chapter are based on
this methodology.

Chapter 6

Discussion in this chapter is based on state-wise estimates
of area irrigated, compiled by the Ministry of Agriculture.
Interregional inequality in access to both surface and
groundwater irrigation sources has declined progressively
over the last four decades. This reduction is more marked in
the case of surface irrigation than with groundwater.

Data on the proportion of area operated that is irrigated in different size classes of holdings are available from the decennial surveys of landholdings and cultivation conducted by the National Sample Survey. It shows that while this proportion has increased in all size classes, the increase in smaller-sized holdings is much smaller compared to those of larger size. Larger-sized holdings have benefited much more from the overall expansion of irrigation than small ones.

Deficiencies in the design and implementation of programmes, watershed development, and agricultural improvement of rainfed areas, are discussed in the official Eleventh Five Year Plan document, and by a special working group for the preparation of the Twelfth Plan. These are accessible on http://planningcommission.nic.in, last accessed in August 2012.

Chapter 7

For recent reviews of the sources of water scarcity, the diverse conflicts over water in specific cases within India, Europe, and the USA, the manner in which they have been tackled, the mechanisms used and their effectiveness, see Ramaswamy Iyer, R. (2007), *Towards Water Wisdom: Limits, Justice, Harmony*. New Delhi: Sage Publications; Vaidyanathan, A. and H.M. Oudshoorn [eds] (2004),

Managing Water Scarcity—Experience and Prospects. New Delhi: Manohar Publishers; World Bank (1991), *India Irrigation Sector Review.* Washington D.C.: World Bank.

Chapter 8

For more details on the topics covered in this chapter, refer to:

Government of India (1992), *Report of the Committee on Pricing of Irrigation Water for a Comprehensive Programme of Legal, Institutional, and Economic Reforms for Better Management of Water.* New Delhi: Planning Commission.

Report of the Working Group on Water Database Development and Management for the 12th Five Year Plan (2012–2017), available at http://planningcommission.nic.in/aboutus/committee/workgrp12/wr/wg-data.pdf, last accessed in August 2012.

Vaidyanathan, A. (2003), 'Interlinking of Peninsular Rivers: A Critique', *Economic and Political Weekly*, 38 (27).

Index

access to water 113, 116,
119–22
agricultural: development
26, 39; productivity xxiv,
43, 77, 79, 103, 202;
technology 77
agriculture xix, xxv, xxxiii,
xxxvi, 3, 20, 44, 51–2, 77,
109, 111, 114, 123, 133;
electricity tariffs for 108;
free power for 106, 108;
groundwater for 165;
illegal appropriation of
water for 135; polluted
water and 138; power
consumption for 108;
unrecovered costs on
109; water requirements
of 147
agro-climatic conditions 15,
58, 70, 161, 186
allocation of water 27,
135, 192, 203–4, 211;
American system of
130; rules for 94, 98,
175
aquifers xx–xxi, 115, 129,
137, 201; of Indo-
Gangetic plains 114;
zones of xxi
augmentation 146–8; of
drinking water supply
27; of utilizable water
148